The Event Horse

The author with 'Fair and Square' competing in the dressage phase of the Badminton Three Day Event. The movement shows horse and rider moving from left to right at the half-pass and is a perfect example of attitude and direction.

The Event Horse

SHEILA WILLCOX

J. B. Lippincott Company
Philadelphia and New York

Copyright © 1973 by Sheila Willcox

Printed in Great Britain

Reprinted 1976
Reprinted 1978

U.S. Library of Congress Cataloging in Publication Data

Willcox, Sheila.
   The event horse..

1. Show riding.   2. Show jumping.
3. Three-day event (Horsemanship).   4. Horse-training.
I. Title.
SF295.2.W55   636.1′08′88   73-5923
ISBN-0-397-01000-1

To Captain Edy Goldman
as a salute to his artistry and consummate skill
and to his unsurpassed record as a trainer

Acknowledgements

My best thanks to Miss Judy Bradwell and Mrs Molly Sievewright for giving up their valuable time to act as models for the photographs, and to Miss Marjorie Whitehurst for producing the drawings, etc.

Contents

Illustrations

PHOTOGRAPHS

DRAWINGS

BY HER ROYAL HIGHNESS THE PRINCESS ANNE

Countless books have been written on or about the horse—its history, breeds, education, you name it and somebody has written about it and usually illustrated some part of the horse's many talents. There have been books on dressage, on jumping, on polo, but to my certain knowledge there has never been a comprehensive book on the specific requirements of the event horse. I can think of no one better qualified to write such a book than Sheila Willcox. Packed into it is seventeen years of Horse Trials experience— presented in the simplest of terms and yet covering everything that the budding event rider and the more experienced riders could ever wish to know.

Sheila's tragic accident in 1971 was a great loss to eventing, but she has turned it into a great gain for the sport in another way by taking the time and thought to create this guide. I feel that the world of Horse Trials will owe her a debt of gratitude for many years to come for her contribution to the continuation and improvement of the Event Horse.

Anne

Introduction

The purpose of this book is to provide a guide to the whole preparation of an event horse. It has been written with the intention of interesting and of helping not only the few who are determined to reach the top but also the great majority who wish to train themselves and their horses simply to the best of their ability.

The book deals with all aspects of eventing, from the actual choice of a horse through to participation in a Three-Day-Event. It covers the basic and systematic work on the ground, the necessary jumping exercises and practice, and it advises on the all-important and often neglected aspects of horsemastership and stable-management. It gives a detailed timetable of the training programme in preparation for a Trials' season, including fast work as well as the daily dressage and graduated long exercise. The final chapters introduce the rider firstly to the routine and approach at a One-Day-Event and, lastly, at the more demanding Three-Day-Event.

The experience I have gained during the years of competition in Trials from 1954 to 1971 is the greatest contributor to this book. The method of training I have evolved is based entirely on common sense and written so that either an experienced or an inexperienced rider will understand clearly what is advised and feel capable of putting it into practice.

CHAPTER ONE
The Horse

There is no set pattern. The best Event horses come in all shapes and sizes; but they all have several qualities in common. The main requirements are courage, stamina, jumping ability, a sensible temperament and absolute soundness, and although there have been a few top class Eventers around 15 hands, it is much more sensible to start with something bigger. The ideal is 16·1 h.h. to 16·3 h.h., with good flat bone, straight movement and conformation suitable for a working hunter championship qualifier. Remember to look also for a horse with presence and plenty of room between the eyes to denote character and intelligence. Again, some of the good horses have been excitable in temperament but as a rule these have had to overcome a poor dressage mark with fast and brilliant jumping over the cross-country. This is good enough to win on occasions, but the whole object of this book is to show how to produce a horse which excels in all three phases of first a One-Day-Event and then a Three-Day-Event, and for that reason I maintain that temperament is a most important ingredient. You must aim for a horse which needs perhaps half an hour's riding-in before his test, instead of being forced to join those riders who have to be out one, or even two, hours before producing anything like a good test. This training programme bears in mind throughout the ultimate demands of a Three-Day-Event and the necessity of having a well-trained and obedient horse even though he is at peak fitness and feeling at his exhilarated best. I have used it on many different horses, and always with the same success as far as the method is concerned.

Having found a horse with the right looks and action, then you have to make sure he can jump. Again, the idea is to buy a horse of five or six years old, and preferably one which has been hunted, for in this case he will have learned to look after himself and to act in all sorts of going. Buying a younger horse is more of a gamble, for one should not ask a three- or four-year-old suddenly to face a big fence. Whilst it is possible when seeing a horse for the first time to assess his jumping potential over a smaller obstacle, it is not as satisfactory as knowing the horse goes hunting really well. On the debit side, the five- or six-year-old with the required experience may have been ridden in a manner totally different from the way in which you will want him to go and this may well provide considerable difficulties, whereas in the case of a three- or four-year-old the entire training is in your hands from the start. The risk, however, remains infinitely greater with the younger horse as, firstly, you take more of a chance with his jumping potential and, secondly, there is a far greater time lag before you can decide whether or not he is the right material for the job, or can hope to compete. A horse has to be at least five years old before taking part in his first One-Day-Event above the Training Level, and if the animal has outstanding potential, he may well be too immature to compete at five and will benefit enormously by waiting until he is five-and-a-half or six before making his Trials' debut.

I shall refer to the horse as 'him' throughout the book, because all my own Event horses have been geldings. Certainly, there are some very good mares in Eventing, and they have the advantage over a gelding in the case of breaking down or of developing an unsoundness. The gelding at once becomes useless except for light exercise after a considerable period of treatment and convalescence, but the mare, especially if she has been successful, is a potential for breeding and accordingly still retains a certain value. My personal preference has been for geldings simply because they are generally more reliable and consistent than mares. In a sport where frequent participation is impossible owing to the demands and rigours of the actual Event, this is a very important factor.

The training of an Event horse throughout the various stages to the ultimate perfect article is a great responsibility and challenge. The whole aim is to produce a horse schooled to medium dressage standard, with good, basic paces and extensions and able to perform accurately and easily the more advanced movements of counter canter, work on two tracks, and pirouettes at the walk. Above all, the horse must have attained the second stage of dressage training: self carriage. His hind legs must be well under him and his forehand light and free. His basic paces must be pure at all times and he must be perfectly straight. He must achieve outstanding rhythm, bordering on cadence. He must show correct length bend and be accurate and obedient. Most important of all, he must do this with presence and show that he enjoys his work and that he neither resents nor begrudges his whole-hearted co-operation. It is perfectly possible to train a horse to this standard without boring him in the process, and it is a poor tribute to dressage trainers that so many people believe a horse schooled for dressage becomes too set and stilted for the rider's genuine enjoyment. My aim is to have a horse which is an absolute delight to ride. Easy to manœuvre because he is light in hand and immediately responsive to the slightest aid. I do not want an automaton but a confident, free-striding and happy horse with whom I can communicate and merge into a perfect partnership.

A confident, free-striding and happy horse. The horse is patently enjoying his work and strides forward frankly.

In the following chapters I shall explain my method of training from the moment we have a suitable horse with potential, through the various stages of work on the ground, through the jumping preparation and the actual programme of getting the horse fit for an Event, to the ultimate objective of participation in a Three-Day-Event. I stress also the great importance of the well-being of the horse, the necessity of a strict timetable and the careful supervision of diet and stable management. There is no point too small to be ignored, nor must anything become too much trouble if you are to reach the top. It is up to you.

CHAPTER TWO

The Rider

The Trials rider is almost of equal importance with the horse. I say 'almost' on purpose, as it is perfectly obvious by looking at the records over a number of years that certain combinations of horse and rider have been outstandingly successful. Nevertheless, that same rider never produces a second really good horse, and newcomers to the game, assessing the rider on current form with a new horse, are at a loss to understand how he or she could have been such a success. The answer is extremely simple. There are several really outstanding horses who would be equally successful with any competent rider aboard, and it is sheer good luck if one of these happens to be your horse. Any reasonably good rider can produce one superb horse in a career, but the element of luck is superseded by real talent if he manages to repeat the success with subsequent animals.

The aim of a good rider is to try to improve daily and never to imagine there is nothing left to learn. Schooling horses is a marvellous test of character, for it requires great tact and patience coupled with the ability to discriminate between an awkward, uncooperative horse and one who simply does not understand. The final product is testimony to the trainer's artistry and if the horse emerges as a well-schooled animal, obedient and calm in his work but patently happy and willing, the trainer has done a good job. You should realise from the start that a bad horse is made; he is never born that way. It is up to you to make the best use of the horse's innate qualities and virtues and to use your own common-sense to solve the problems which will inevitably arise during the training.

The horse is by nature a nervous creature who will run rather than fight, and he has no conception of his strength and size until circumstances prove this to him. Once you accept this fact and realise its implications you will appreciate the great responsibility you undertake when training a horse. His size alone magnifies his mistakes, and his slightest clumsy action may result in him being punished unfairly when he cannot understand what he has done wrong. If he treads on your foot or swishes you in the eye with his tail he cannot possibly realise what he has done, and if he is then punished he will only become nervous and more liable to get himself into trouble. You must avoid bullying the horse or trying to dominate him to such an extent that eventually he begins seriously to resist. Resistance can lead to the realisation of his strength and your consequent inability to match it. Many good horses are spoilt in this way. It is your job to treat the horse fairly in all circumstances and to produce him ultimately as a co-operative and happy animal using his strength and power confidently in the correct channels.

Any shortcomings in the trainer's approach will be revealed in the horse's work, and if you lose your temper or are unable to be consistent in your aids, you will inevitably produce an unhappy horse which has little confidence and is apt to 'blow up' at the slightest provocation. If you are thinking seriously of riding in Trials, you should be aware that a great deal of talent and application is required to reach the top. Also it is necessary to spend much time in the preparation and training for the Events, and if you happen to be groom as well as rider, it becomes virtually a full-time job.

There are many competitors, of course, who have no ambition other than to be able to take part in novice events, and to enjoy that participation with no real aim of great success. But they too will benefit from a proper preparation and will derive infinitely more enjoyment from riding a well-trained and fit horse. Another consideration is temperament. Some riders will never have the patience for the systematic training, nor will they wish to spend the time in preparing a horse for Eventing. After all, the training is only one facet of the sport, and the process of getting a horse fit is even more time-consuming. It is very much easier and quicker to school a horse for show jumping, and this may appeal to many riders with a gift of timing, especially if they are lucky enough to find a horse capable of jumping the big fences cleanly. Horse Trials are for the all-rounder, someone who wishes to excel not just in one sphere but in all three. They present a competition which associates exceptionally well with hunting, as riders who go well to hounds have the great advantage of having learned to ride across a country from an early age.

The rider's influence is obviously of paramount importance from the earliest days of training, and you must develop great feeling so that you can anticipate the horse's difficulties and deal immediately with them. Your position on the horse must be such that your body and legs are able to exert the greatest influence.

Your position on the horse. The perfect seat, marred only by a slight forwards and downwards tilt of the rider's head.

The back must be strong and straight, the head held high but easily, and there must be no tendency to look to one side—a common fault—or to sit on one side with a collapsed hip. The back is the very essence of the seat, and if you look down or lean forward the back cannot be used. You cannot feel the horse, nor appreciate the rhythm and cadence. If you lean forward, the weight shifts to the forehand, and the horse starts to run. Your thighs should lie easily at such an angle to the body that the lower leg rests just behind the girth and the back of the heel is in a straight line with the body. The lower legs are in a position to act on the motor nerves when applied behind the girth, and they act on the sensory nerves in achieving 'combined effect'—the only time they are applied on the girth. The legs should never be used to kick at the horse but always act as a pressure aid to a greater or lesser extent as required. The heel should be well down and the foot turned out only slightly away from the line of the leg. The stirrup rests on the ball of the foot. Your upper arm rests naturally and loosely against your body and the lower arm forms a straight line from elbow to the horse's mouth.

Some riders, even successful ones, fail to realise how incorrectly they sit, and for this reason they cannot act on the horse to the best advantage. They use far more strength than is necessary and wonder why they are so tired. Many sit to one side with a collapsed hip, and others persist in carrying their heads, and consequently their weight, to a certain extent to one side. You could learn a salutary lesson by watching a cinematic film of yourself riding from time to time.

The horse progresses along a corridor made up of the rider's hands and legs. The rider's legs create impulsion, or the generating power from behind, the hands control it and distribute it. The hands must be at all times sympathetic and responsive. It is their responsibility to open or close only to the fractional degree required for a movement, and to be perfectly co-ordinated with the rider's legs and weight. They must never be used in a backward movement to stop the horse—who must learn to go forward when the hand relaxes or 'opens', and to slow down or stop according to the degree of the 'closing' of the hand. As soon as the horse deviates from the straight line you take your hands apart and adjust the horse's forehand to the quarters; always the forehand to the quarters, as the horse is narrower in front than behind and it is easier for him to adjust in this way.

Good hands are a gift, but every rider should concentrate on developing hands as sympathetic as possible. You should vow never to jag the horse in the mouth, for this is an unforgivable sin, committed by the ignorant or the ill-tempered. The horse becomes afraid of the action of the bit instead of accepting it happily, and his mouth will become sore as a result of a cruel or impatient jag.

The action of the hands is very important and you must learn to keep them quiet yet sensitive and not to allow them to move up and down with the movement of your body. They are carried at the same angle as when reaching out to shake hands. They must not be held rigid or twisted from the wrist, either with the palms facing down or facing up. The thumb is on top and rests on the first finger. The fingers are the vehicle for opening and closing the hand. You clench your hand gently to 'close' the hand—fingers curving into and touching the palms. As the hand 'opens' the fingers are less bent and much more pliable. The fingers are used to vibrate the reins and they act to keep the horse's mouth super-sensitive and to attract his attention.

You must studiously avoid the temptation of pulling back at the horse whenever he pulls at you. This only results in a 'dead' mouth. You must learn the degree to 'give' to the horse so that he finds he has nothing to lean on and cannot be supported in this way. On the other hand, he must be encouraged to keep his head and neck in the position consistent with the stage of his training. Make him realise that you will not pull against him when he pulls at you. Instead, after the momentary 'giving' of the hand, you will use your legs to drive him up to the bit and close the hand whilst vibrating the fingers so that he does not resent the action. He will relax his jaw happily, lower his head and become lighter and more responsive.

You must learn to keep your temper and remain calm, whatever the provocation, for you will gain nothing but an upset and confused horse by punishing him indiscriminately in a few moments of rage. The main thing to remember is that the horse is like a child; he needs firm but sympathetic handling and he needs to feel secure. He will take advantage of you if he thinks he can get away with it, so he must learn a certain amount of respect. Throughout the training you must bear this in mind. Your aids and instructions must be clear at all times, leaving the horse with no excuse for disobedience. He must learn that co-operation is pleasant and that disobedience will be dealt with firmly; that ultimately he will have to do what you want.

The whole aim is for the rider to look as if he is part of the horse. He should sit easily and confidently and give the impression he is merely a passenger and that the horse is performing brilliantly of his own initiative. In actual fact the rider is dictating every fractional movement of the horse, but the aids are so slight and delicate as to be invisible even to a knowledgeable observer. When the onlooker decides the whole thing looks so easy that he could do it himself, you have gone far towards the ultimate goal of perfection.

CHAPTER THREE

The Arena—its size and shape
The school figures

In order to follow the book more easily, you should study the diagrams of the school figures contained in this chapter. You will then have no difficulty in envisaging the various exercises in relation to the arena and find it very much easier to put them into immediate practice.

The arena is referred to as such as a further simplification but it may be an indoor school, an outdoor manège or just a flat field. In the latter case it is important to work on good ground and it will help you to be more correct and accurate if you enclose the working area with dressage boards or some other suitable material. At the very least, you can define the right-angles of the four corners with planks tilted on their side and supported behind with bricks, and you can mark the centre and quarter markers with bamboo canes or small posts.

'A' is your point of entry so you mark this as in a dressage arena with two canes one metre either side of A, leaving plenty of room to enter on a straight line accurately on the marker. Later on you can define the centre line, and the markers X and G with a mowed or raked strip, depending on the footing. The horse must be able to follow exactly the track of a marked line before he makes his debut in the public dressage arena and this is very much more difficult than you imagine. He may be suspicious of the mowed or raked strip at first and may even shy at the cross and large circle marking X and G. He must be given plenty of time and opportunity to grow used to this.

The bottom of the arena is always where A is situated. The top end of the arena has C as its centre. The quarter markers are six metres in from each corner on the long side of the arena. This applies both to the 40 metres × 20 metres arena and the 60 metres × 20 metres arena. The centre markers of A, C, E and B are at the middle points of the short and long sides of the arena. X is the middle point between A and C and E and B. G is six metres from C and the middle point between H and M.

In the early lessons you will need to extend the size of your arena and it may become 60 metres × 30 metres. This gives the horse more space at a time when he is incapable of responding immediately to your aids and finds it difficult to remain on a twenty metre circle.

Riding correctly in an arena means that the horse is perfectly straight on the outside track and goes well into the corners. There is no such thing as just riding once round the arena without any problems. Even a simple circuit of the arena provides seventeen specific problems for horse and rider. At each of the four corners, attention must be paid first to the positioning of the horse; second to maintaining the length bend; and third to straightening the horse. On each of the four sides the horse must be kept straight, and throughout the circuit the even footfall and rhythm must remain unaltered.

The actual school figures are as follows:

1. *The Circles.* In the two official size arenas, 60 metres × 20 metres and 40 metres × 20 metres, there are three accepted circles of 20 metres. The first starts at C which becomes the first tangent;

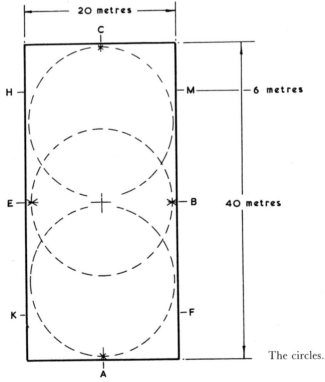

The circles.

the second tangent is on the long side of the arena ten metres in from the corner; the third is at X if the arena measures 40 metres × 20 metres, or on the centre line twenty metres in from A if the arena is 60 metres × 20 metres; and the fourth is on the second long side ten metres in from the bottom corner of the arena.

The second circle has its centre at X and its first and third tangents on the centre-markers of each long side. The second and fourth tangents are on the centre line from A to C ten metres either side of X.

The third circle is at the top end of the arena. The first tangent is at C; the second ten metres down from the corner on the long side; the third on the centre line (A to C) twenty metres from C; and the fourth on the long side of the arena ten metres down from the top corner.

Riding a circle correctly requires that the horse does not go into the corners as he would when going round the arena. Immediately on starting the circle he moves away from the outside track. The true circle touches the tangents of the circle for only four strides at the trot and three at the canter, and it is impossible to ride it perfectly unless the horse is continually on the curve and the rider is looking for the next tangent as he approaches its predecessor.

2. *Up or down the centre line.* This is self explanatory but the horse must travel in an absolutely straight line from A to C or from C to A. He must turn before the marker to merge with the centre line and the rider must guard against the horse swinging off the line as he prepares to turn at the far end.

3. *Doubler.* This figure may be executed either along the centre line A to C or along the line from E to B. The horse progresses along the required line and turns at the next marker so that he remains on the same rein. The horse must show a perfect turn with no escape of the quarters, then he must be straight, and lastly, he must complete a second turn showing length bend on the correct arc.

Doubler, and change the rein, means that the horse, having turned at the required marker, changes the rein at the next marker. It demands a definite change of bend.

4. *Change of rein across the diagonal.* Riding round the arena the rider changes the rein from the first quarter marker on one side of the arena to the second quarter marker on the other passing over X at the centre. Again, the figure demands a change of bend.

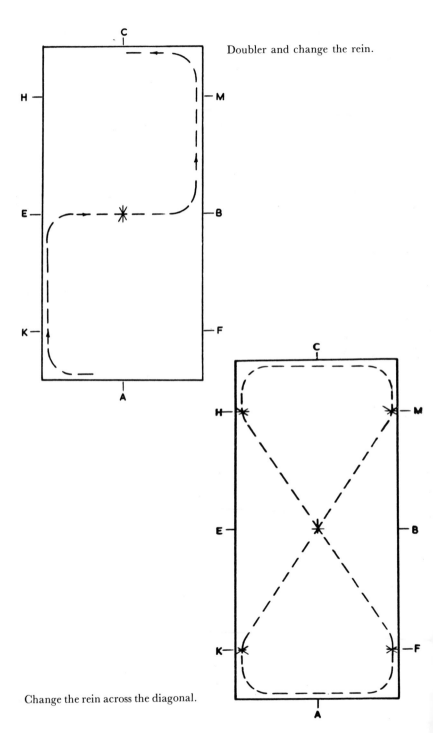

Doubler and change the rein.

Change the rein across the diagonal.

Counter change of hand.

Change of rein within the circle.

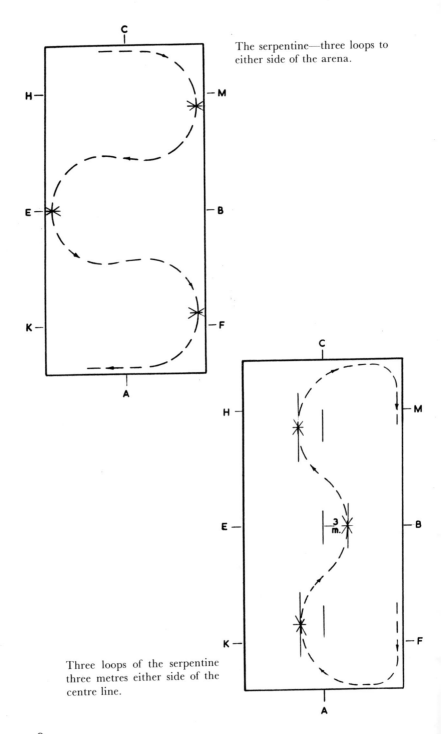

The serpentine—three loops to either side of the arena.

Three loops of the serpentine three metres either side of the centre line.

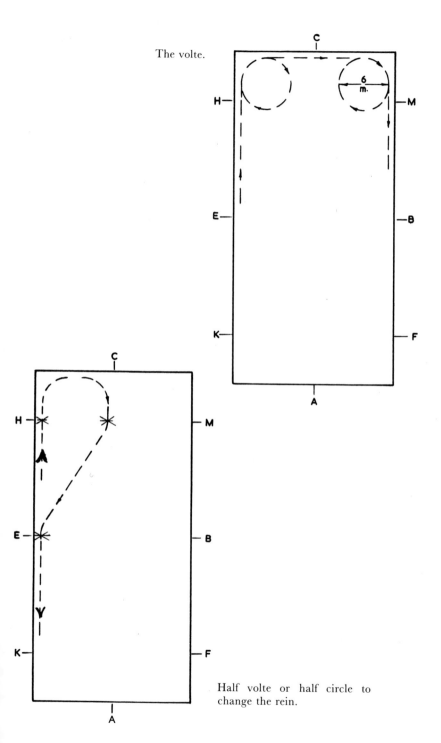

The volte.

Half volte or half circle to change the rein.

5. *Counter change of hand.* There is no change of rein here, but the figure provides changes of bend at two markers. The horse is ridden from the first quarter marker on the long side of the arena towards X and then back to the second quarter marker on the same long side.

6. *Change of rein within the circle.* Another method of changing the rein. The horse moves smoothly from one length bend to the other.

7. *The Serpentine.* An exercise to demonstrate changes of bend and accurate and even loops. The horse must retain perfect rhythm and impulsion throughout the movement.

8. *Volte.* The volte is any circle that measures less than six metres. It can be executed either in the corners of the arena of from any straight line.

9. *Half volte.* A useful figure for changing the rein from the corner of the arena or anywhere on the long side of the arena. The horse shows perfect length bend whilst describing the half circle, becomes absolutely straight on his track back to the long side of the arena and then shows the change of bend as he reaches the outside track and is changing the rein. It is also of particular benefit during work at the half pass as the half circle helps the horse to assume the correct position before he moves obliquely back to the long side of the arena on two tracks.

CHAPTER FOUR

General directive. The three stages of training.
Free, forward movement. The correct circle. Length
bend. The half halt. Transitions: halt—walk—trot

The first step in the training programme is to achieve a certain standard of obedience. You will need this before you can begin to teach the horse the correct way to jump rather than allowing him to jump with natural talent only and without using himself to the best of his ability. Assuming the horse has hunted or that you know he jumps well, forget that side of the preparation and concentrate entirely on ground work to ensure this obedience.

From the very first moment make the difference between right and wrong abundantly clear to the horse, using the voice as an aid, making much of the horse when he does right and saying a firm and decided 'No' when he makes a mistake. This 'No' becomes very useful on all sorts of occasions. Later on, the mere utterance of the word will be enough to stop the horse doing whatever is wrong. It applies not only to when he is being ridden but also to him in the stable and at any other time. It is your indication that he has made a mistake and must correct it immediately.

It is important for your aids always to be absolutely consistent and crystal clear, and that any new lesson you wish to teach the horse is carefully explained. Above all you must avoid confusion, because a confused horse, especially if he is an obliging sort and wants to please, will offer all sorts of movements in the hope of producing the right answer; he will then progress from confusion and fear to a complete mental and physical block.

The horse is first and foremost a creature of habit and has a remarkable memory. You must make the best use of these virtues and channel them to your own advantage. He is a gentle animal by nature, spoiled only by bad treatment or careless training. In these cases he develops, through utter self defence, evasions which soon become bad habits and which may be difficult to eradicate. It is the rider's responsibility to try to minimise the times of misunderstanding and never to ask too much of the horse in his early training. One lesson must be fully understood before the next is undertaken, and your aim the whole time should be to make the process interesting and easily understood.

The importance of this elementary work on the ground is twofold: firstly, it forms the sound basis of good dressage and, secondly, it will simplify and help the jumping tuition. Many horses are very keen to jump: but it is not enough just to get to the other side of a fence. The objective is to produce a horse who is cool and calm in his jumping, who uses himself to the highest degree of his athletic ability and is easily adaptable to the pace you dictate. For this, you will need complete obedience.

Dressage is the phase of Eventing where you know exactly what is required, and it is therefore poor policy not to take the greatest advantage of this. The basic paces of walk, trot and canter are the first considerations and they must become one hundred per cent pure and in strict four-time, two-time and three-time respectively. This is not as simple and straightforward as it sounds for it is all too easy for an unlevel trot or 'bridle lameness' to develop, and if you insist on too slow a canter at too early a stage it will lapse into four-time and become a glaring fault. Throughout the training, emphasis must be laid on forward movement. The horse must go freely forward and with developing impulsion and should give the impression of great activity and strength in all paces. This strength and activity will develop from the progressively increasing use of the hind leg. The hind leg is the horse's motor and it creates the force of energy and impulsion from behind.

In the first of the three stages of work on the ground the horse will be in the long and low position. The head and neck must be low and stretched. He must learn to use his hocks and to push freely forward from behind. The centre of gravity is over the forehand at this stage, but as the systematic training progresses this centre of gravity will shift further back until ultimately the quarters are lower than the forehand, the hind leg is firmly engaged well under the horse and he carries his full weight on his hocks. The Three-Day-Event horse must have gained not only 'self-carriage'—which is the second stage of training—but to a certain extent the third stage, the 'carrying capacity of the hocks'. Conformation and temperament obviously play a great part in the degree of perfection which any horse may achieve in dressage but it is an undoubted fact that any horse will benefit enormously from the training. In just the same way as an athlete's performance improves as his body becomes perfectly attuned, so will the systematically-trained horse—even of limited physique—improve out of all recognition. It is a rewarding and fascinating process.

The first step is to develop the propelling power of the hocks. The horse must learn to use his hocks and to push freely forwards from behind. His head and neck must be low and stretched to enable him to do this. His centre of gravity inevitably is over the forehand. The work takes place on level land, preferably not too open, but it will be all to the good if there are distractions in the form of passing traffic and other everyday occurrences. An indoor school is an invaluable asset, but its constant use has many dangers and drawbacks, and the rider is apt to forget that his horse must perform equally well in many different circumstances of weather and location. If the horse has been accustomed to working only indoors he will inevitably fail to reproduce that same form outside when facing the elements and without a supporting wall.

The rider chooses to work in a rectangular area, approximately 60 yards × 30 yards. This allows plenty of room for the unschooled horse who as yet is incapable of maintaining any sort of rhythm in a confined area. You begin by making sure the horse is straight. This means that the axis of the horse is adapted to the track he is following whether it be a straight line or a curved one. On a straight line the horse must be straight and on a curve he must bend correctly along the curved line of the corner, the turn or the circle, his hind legs following exactly in the track of the front legs.

The trot pace is the easiest at which to start work as it is a diagonal movement in two-time. In order to prevent any early inclination to unlevel work at the rising trot the rider must be sure to sit equally on both diagonals whether he be schooling the horse or simply riding out. Every horse has a distinct preference for one diagonal and will 'throw' the rider so that he sits down when the favoured hind leg meets the ground. He must learn to accept the rider's weight just as happily on the one side as the other but for work in the arena it is best to sit when the inside hind leg meets the ground. This will activate the inside hind leg which becomes the driving force on any curved line.

The rider asks the horse to trot actively around the arena, using his legs with equal pressure to drive the horse forward. His hands control the forward movement, preventing the horse from going too fast so that the creative energy bounces back from the hand to the hind leg where first it was generated. It is this constant use of creating and maintaining the free forward movement that will eventually develop into true impulsion. The horse works in the arena through all the school figures of turns, circles, half voltes—a means of changing the rein—doublers and counter changes of hand.

The circle is a very important and useful figure and the rider must learn to ride it correctly so that it can be used to the greatest advantage. The best places for using the circle in the arena are at the top end, the bottom end, and the middle. The first attempt should always be made at one of the ends—for we have three sides of the arena to provide the points of the tangents. A true circle is described by drawing a line representing the required diameter of the circle along the centre line of the arena from the top marker. At the middle of this line another of the same diameter is drawn at right angles and the resulting four ends become the tangents of the circle.

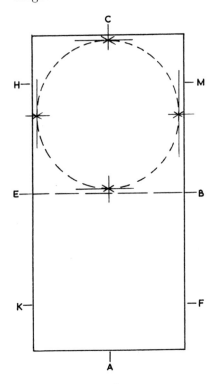

How to ride a correct twenty-metre circle, showing the four tangents.

THE CORRECT CIRCLE

Riding a circle correctly means that the horse, following the continual curve of the circle, touches the four tangents for only four strides at the trot and three at the canter. The rider's weight on the circle is slightly on the inside seatbone. The outside hip and outside shoulder are slightly forward, so that the rider's shoulders are parallel to those of the horse. The rider's inside leg is applied just behind the girth and the outside leg a little further back. A green horse will find it difficult to describe a correct circle, so the rider should begin by using lateral aids, taking his inside rein towards the centre of the circle to encourage the horse to a continual turn, and using his inside leg to keep the horse out on the circle. You want the horse to feel the inside rein and to give to it so that he flexes naturally and easily to the inside. As soon as he learns this lesson, you will need to be able to control the size of the circle and this you do by using the outside rein combined with the inside leg. The inside leg keeps the horse from falling in on the circle while the outside rein dictates the size of it. The inside rein, carried always towards the centre of the circle, and with no backward tension, gives the correct bend and flexion whenever it is required. Eventually the horse is able to describe a perfect circle, with the rider's weight and influence perfectly distributed and co-ordinated. He must learn to trot in even rhythm around the arena and to circle at either end or in the centre with equal facility to left and right.

Most horses are one-sided and find it easier to go on one rein than the other but the weaker side is soon apparent and it is then a matter of practice until the horse becomes equally at home on either rein. Never trot round and round the arena or continue on the circle until the horse is drooping with boredom. He will work happily at his daily lessons as long as the rider is tactful enough to vary the content of the programme. The horse will remain interested if he is continually changing direction and pace and has every new lesson explained clearly so that there is no room for confusion. Should he not understand what is required of him at any time and become patently upset with the rider's attempts to enforce the lesson it is almost certain that the rider is at fault. You must never allow the horse to become upset, and if this happens it is because your aids have not been clear enough or because you have shown a complete lack of feeling and sympathy.

You must be able to differentiate between a naughty horse and a confused one. While the former will need firm treatment and in some cases a real battle of wills, the latter needs calming and reassuring before the lesson can be continued.

The walk is an invaluable aid to restore calm, and the horse should learn from the start to walk on a free rein with his head low and stretched. As the dressage training progresses the daily programme should be punctuated often by short spells of this relaxed walk. It will eliminate any tendency to tension and give the horse an opportunity to rest and stretch his neck and back muscles.

Most of the earliest work is done at the trot until the horse can circle and change direction without losing his rhythm and can

Length bend in the corner of the arena. The horse's body is a little too tilted inwards but the picture shows clearly the continual curve throughout the length of his body.

Length bend on a circle. The hind feet are following exactly in the tracks of the fore feet, whilst the horse's body is bent on the continual curve.

Length bend as the horse turns down the centre line, merging with the line and not over-lapping it. In the next stride the horse will be completely straight on the centre line.

maintain his straightness along the sides of the arena, through the corners and turns, and on a circle. Just as you ask the horse to show some inside flexion whilst on a circle, although still remaining straight, so it is when riding a corner. The horse must be placed in position as he approaches the corner, first by a warning half halt—a momentary closing of hands and legs—and then by the rider feeling the inside rein with a vibrating movement of the fingers. The inside leg comes into play at the start of the corner, the outside rein controls the curve of the corner, and lastly the outside leg prevents the horse's quarters from swinging out and then straightens the horse as he reaches the long side. The horse is bent round the rider's inside leg. This is length bend.

THE HALF HALT

The half halt is in effect a warning to the horse and you will continue to use this aid throughout the horse's training as a signal to him to expect an immediate instruction. The half halt is obtained by closing the legs on the girth and closing the hands momentarily to form a wall. The hind legs come under the horse, the forehand is elevated slightly and the quarters lowered correspondingly. The centre of gravity shifts to the quarters and the horse becomes immediately attentive, ready and able to perform a new movement or transition. The half halt cannot work unless the horse is straight, and this straightness is of paramount importance. The horse must be straight before you can get him on the bit and develop free forward movement or impulsion. The rider's hands and legs combine sympathetically to get the horse on the bit or to achieve what is called direct flexion.

The horse's mouth is sensitive and you want to keep it that way. You must not allow it to become dead and unresponsive—the inevitable result of harsh and unsympathetic hands. The rein forms the contact between the horse's mouth and the rider's hands and this rein must become and remain a living, vibrant thing. The rider must learn to 'give' with the hand as soon as he feels the horse flex, and in this way the horse learns to appreciate the reward and to flex happily and accept his bit. Harsh hands produce backward tension, and the horse's mouth quickly deteriorates until it becomes totally unresponsive. Alternatively he may refuse to take hold of or to accept his bit as he should—simply because he fears the harsh use of the hand. In this case he is 'behind the bit' and will need sympathetic hands and much driving forward before the fault is eliminated. Horses which throw their heads are merely demonstrating their unhappiness against the hands and as often as not the various faults of head tilting are the result of the unequal influence of the hands. The aids to get the horse on the bit are 'combined effect'. The hands are raised with no backward tension and the fingers vibrate gently and evenly. The legs are brought forward on to the girth and vibrate gently and easily on the sensory nerves. As soon as the horse relaxes his jaw and lowers his head, the combined effect is achieved and he is on the bit. The hands are then lowered and the legs revert to their normal position.

TRANSITIONS: HALT-WALK-TROT

You must practice unceasingly to perfect the transitions from halt to walk, walk to trot and the more difficult transitions downwards. The horse must learn always to stand square at the halt, so from the start insist on this by making sure he has a leg truly at each corner whenever you stop. Never pull the horse back a step to correct him but always take a step forward. Be patient, and reward the horse with a pat and a pleased voice when he achieves a good halt. The aids to move into a walk are always preceded by making sure the horse is on the bit with the 'combined effect'. As soon as the horse flexes, relaxes his jaw and lowers his head, he is ready to go forward. The rider immediately closes his legs quietly and easily just behind the girth. The power generated from behind goes forward to the hand, and the hand opens slightly to allow the horse to walk on from behind. If the hand does not give at the right moment the horse's head will go up and he will come off the bit.

In all movements, hand and leg must work perfectly together and the rider must learn to use his weight to influence and help the horse. Having walked on from a halt, concentrate on a good active walk and then ask the horse to trot. The aids are the same: first the warning half halt, then both legs applied behind the girth with equal pressure and a slight opening of the hand to allow the horse to make the transition smoothly and evenly. If the horse persists in throwing his head in the transition it may help to widen and lower the hands as you ask him to trot, always remembering to give with the hand the instant you feel the first trot stride coming. It is also a help to teach the horse the words of command, and you should use clearly defined commands so that the horse cannot be confused. The commands are emphasised WAAaaLK, T-ROT and CAN-TER and the transitions down are the same but preceded by a drawled 'and'. This is where the horse's memory is extremely useful. He soon assimilates these words of command and learns the aids very much more quickly. The voice has an added advantage when the horse is excited or upset, especially when he goes away to compete for the first time. The voice, with its accustomed words of command, soothes him and reassures him at a time when he is supersensitive to your aids and may react too strongly to them until he is settled.

He learns these words of command in the first stages of training, and as the horse becomes more proficient at his work the voice will fade until it is no more than a whisper. It is nevertheless still a very effective and helpful aid throughout the entire training.

The transitions from halt to walk and walk to trot should be practised unceasingly until the horse can make the transitions from one pace to another with fluency and ease and without deviating from a straight line. Make use of the school figures at the same time, cirling, turning and changing direction across the diagonals of the school or along the centre line, and introducing the horse to counter change of hand. This figure is described from a quarter marker on the long side of the arena to the centre X, and back to the next quarter marker. It therefore involves a change of direction at X and requires that the horse changes his bend completely at X and back again at the second quarter marker. The diagonal on which you sit at the trot in this figure is unchanged and you continue to sit when the inside hind leg touches the ground throughout the movement. On the other hand, make sure to change your sitting diagonal at the first quarter marker whenever you change the rein across the diagonal. This makes you sit more strongly for the one stride, helps to straighten the horse and gives impulsion as the horse comes out of the first corner. The transitions down are less easy as the horse is apt to sprawl into a lower pace and if the rider is too rough with his aids the horse comes off the bit or above the bit.

The transition from trot to walk must be effected quietly and smoothly by the rider closing his legs, straightening and strengthening his own back, feeling his seat bones press into the saddle and closing his hand. There must be no backward tension, for this is the cause of an abrupt or rough transition and the horse will show his resentment by throwing his head or falling into a walk. The epitome of a good transition is the ease and smoothness with which the horse progresses from one pace to another, and your aim is to produce a picture which to a layman could only be described as 'oiled'.

The walk to halt transition is achieved in the same way: legs applied just behind the girth with equal pressure, a strong back and seat bones, and the closing of the hand. As soon as the horse halts the rider relaxes his fingers slightly but continues to vibrate them to keep the horse attentive and on the bit. Maintain the halt for a few seconds and then make a transition upwards. It is time to start asking the horse to go from halt to trot and later trot to halt as soon as he is able to do the early transitions with ease and fluency.

This preliminary work of teaching the horse to go freely forward, to bend correctly and to make the various transitions from halt to trot will take several weeks and it is important to concentrate on the paces up to the trot only and not to ask the horse to canter in this early stage. At the end of these first few weeks the horse will be very much more balanced and will find it far easier to canter correctly from the first time of asking. The canter is our next stage.

CHAPTER FIVE

The canter. Aids to canter. Überstreichen. Canter to trot transition

The canter is a three-time pace. The footfall sequence with near fore leading is as follows: (1) off-hind; (2) right diagonal of off-fore and near-hind; (3) near-fore. Then follows a moment of suspension when all four feet are off the ground. The half halt, when applied at the canter, is given on the third footfall, and the hand opens again between the first and second footfalls. If the hand resists after the third footfall, the free forward movement is impeded and the horse breaks. The half halt is applied as the inside shoulder comes forward. The aids to canter are preceded, as always, by the warning half halt. The horse becomes attentive. Raise the inside hand slightly, sit on the inside seatbone and apply the inside leg just behind the girth. The very application of these aids means that the rider's weight is greater on the inside and eventually this weight balance, coupled with the vibration of the raised inside rein, will be enough to make the horse strike off correctly.

At first the horse will not understand what you want him to do and, to make it as easy as possible, ride on a circle at the trot. At this stage it is better to use the corner of the field to form the long and short sides of the arena if you are working in the open. Ride, as it were, on the top circle of the arena so that two of your tangents are against the two angles of the fence. As you approach the first of the two sides, still on a circle, sit to the trot, give a half halt, and then apply the aids to canter.

The horse may strike off immediately into a canter, with the inside foreleg leading as required, and in this case make much of him and proceed to canter on round the circle. More likely than not, he will fail to realise what is wanted, and simply trot faster instead. At once he must be steadied and brought back to an active ordinary trot before the next attempt is made. As further encouragement, the voice is used with the emphasised CAN-TER just as the aids are applied. Further, it may help to emphasise the raising of the inside hand with a vibratory movement of the fingers. This latter aid, combined with the slight shifting of the rider's weight, should be your ultimate aim as the total aids for a canter strike off. It is all so slight as to be utterly invisible to an onlooker, but it is effective and easily appreciated by the horse. Continue to strike off at the canter on the circle until you are sure the horse has learnt the lesson and knows exactly what your aids mean.

Work only in one direction, to the left or to the right, and proceed on the same rein to teach the horse to canter away from the circle and on round the arena. If the horse breaks into a trot, revert to the circle at once before asking him to canter on and as soon as he strikes off correctly make much of him. Each time he makes a mistake say a sharp and determined 'No', but remember never to confuse the horse by applying the aids too suddenly after he has made an initial mistake, particularly when he has struck off on the outside leg instead of the inside one. At this stage of training, always ask the horse to canter with the inside foreleg leading, and not until he reaches the stage of counter canter will he be asked or expected to do otherwise. Your aim is to make quite sure he can strike off into the canter with the inside foreleg leading, both to the right and to the left, and until you know the lesson has been learned on the one rein do not work on the other. After this it is important to work equally on both reins, remembering to show your approval when the horse does well, and to say 'No' when he makes a mistake.

Überstreichen

The canter itself must be developed into an energetic and swinging gait. The horse will break continually if you allow him

Encouraging the horse to lengthen and stretch his neck on the circle and to begin to use his back. The outline is long and low.

to canter too slowly or if the arena is too small for him when first he begins the canter work. He must be encouraged to go freely forward, and if the chosen rectangle is too small it must be enlarged until he can canter easily and his balance is improved. Having made the transition from trot to canter, encourage the horse to lengthen and stretch his neck on the circle and to begin to use his back. This you do by taking forward the outside hand for a space of one or two strides, as if the rein were a piece of elastic. In this way, the horse is brought immediately on to the inside rein, and should lower and stretch his head and neck. The German translation of this movement is 'überstreichen', and it is included in the European advanced tests where the surrender of both hands in one contained and smooth movement over one or two strides is designed to show that the horse has obtained perfect 'self carriage',

Überstreichen. Surrendering the hands at the canter. The horse's head and neck remain in the same position. The horse is in self carriage.

and is being driven truly from behind. He is expected to remain perfectly in position and neither to increase nor decrease his pace. In the elementary stages of training it is used firstly, with the surrender of the outside rein, to bring the horse on to the inside rein and thereby to lower and stretch his neck and, secondly, with the surrender of the inside rein, to regain any lost harmony with the horse. It is an invaluable exercise and is done at the trot or canter.

CANTER TO TROT TRANSITIONS
The transitions down afford considerable difficulty, for the transition depends entirely on the rider's finesse and co-ordination.

43

The perfect transition can only be made if the horse remains in balance—steadily on the bit and completely straight. The rider must apply the aids smoothly and at the split second when the horse can make the transition without being thrown off balance. A simple and inevitably successful aid for the canter to trot transition is the use of the outside rein alone. Cantering with the near-fore leading, you apply the aid on the third footfall of the canter—when the near-fore or leading shoulder begins to come forward. Concentrate first on the sequence of the pace until you are sure of the exact moment you should apply the aid. Decide where you want to make the transition to trot and close the outside hand firmly one pace before your marker. The horse will break immediately from his canter and will do this calmly and smoothly. It is only a matter of practice before you can go from canter to trot with considerable ease.

The preliminary canter work will take perhaps two weeks, and at the end of this time the horse should be able to strike off correctly on either leg, either on a circle or on a straight line. His transitions should be smooth and pure, and he should remain on the bit and be perfectly straight. Once this has been achieved, he is ready for the next stage of training.

CHAPTER SIX

Turns on the forehand. The walk: ordinary walk, free walk and free walk on a loose rein. Turns on the haunches. The rein back

The turns on the forehand and the haunches are very useful and suppling exercises. Although the turn on the forehand is not included in any of the dressage tests, it has several advantages. It will teach the horse to be more manoeuvrable and more conversant with the lateral aids, and is a definite help when opening and shutting gates.

TURN ON THE FOREHAND
You proceed as follows: walk the horse along a track parallel with a straight fence and about one metre away from it. Halt. Make sure the horse is standing square, with a foot at each corner. You are on the left rein and will attempt a turn on the forehand to the right. The hind legs will describe a 180° half circle with the forehand of the horse acting as a pivot. The forelegs in fact, will describe a very small half circle and may even give the impression of stepping back slightly. The main fault is for the forelegs to step forward, with the result that the horse is turning, not on the forehand but on the centre, and this must be avoided. Feel the outside rein, the right rein, so that the horse turns his head and neck slightly to the right. Apply the right leg one hand behind the girth. The fingers of the left hand open to allow the horse his bend to the right. The fence guards his outside. The horse will take a step or two so that his hindquarters move to the left but, in the first efforts, he will assume you are asking him just to about-turn. He will try to move forward and round to the right. Prevent this with a half halt and allow him only one step at a time, making much of him when you feel a full step taken with the hind legs whilst the forelegs move only on the spot. The outside hind leg must cross in front of the inside hind leg. Continue the turn one step at a time until it is completed. Walk on—you will now be on the right rein. Make a half circle or half volte, returning to the left rein, and start again. Eventually the horse will understand the aids and be able to

perform the first 90° of the turn steadily and accurately. Do not attempt to hurry him, as this will result only in an incorrect turn. If he makes a mistake, walk on out of the turn, circle, and return to the place where you first started for the next attempt.

It requires patience to produce a perfect turn on the forehand and the lesson must not be hurried as it is very easy to upset or to confuse the horse. Concentrate on the turn to the right until it is thoroughly understood and then repeat the lesson for the turn to the left. In this case you will be on the right rein, the horse's head inclines left, and his quarters move to the right.

THE WALK

This is a good opportunity to work on the horse's walk, as it is the obvious pace to use between turns. The walk is a pace all too often neglected, whereas it needs a great deal of attention. It will assume a twofold value if worked on at this stage. Firstly, it makes the rider concentrate on the walk and to think of it as a pace in itself. It is too easy to dismiss it as unimportant and to think that any horse can walk properly without the necessity of being schooled at it. It is also very easy to use the walk merely as an interval between movements or as a preparation for them. This has the inevitable result of the horse beginning to anticipate as soon as he makes the transition to walk, and his walk inevitably loses its rhythm and purity.

The walk must be confirmed as a pure pace and, in just the same way as in the trot and the canter, this will not happen without application. It is a four-time pace with a footfall as follows: near-hind; near-fore; off-hind; off-fore. The hoofbeats are heard clearly:—one-two-three-four—at precise and equal intervals.

The ordinary walk is the horse's natural pace. He is ridden on a rein of moderate length with steady and positive contact. It is important to realise that the horse must never be forced or pulled into a collected position. This is a particular temptation at the walk as it is comparatively easy to pull in and to raise the head, thereby giving the impression of collection. This impression is completely false. True collection is achieved solely by increasing the activity of the hindlegs, by progressing through the first stage of training—the long and low position—where the horse learns to develop the propelling power of the hocks, to the second stage of training—self carriage. There is no short cut to collection and if the rider tries to enforce it at an early stage, it will result in a complete loss of rhythm. The horse is unable to use his shoulder because head and neck are pulled back to the body and the free, forward movement is consequently impaired. The emphasis must be on forward movement and in the walk, as in the trot and the canter, it is vitally important to drive the horse up from behind and not to pull the horse's head back to his body.

The horse's carriage at the ordinary walk will develop and improve as his work at the trot progresses. The trot, because it is two-time, is the easiest pace for the horse to maintain his balance and rhythm, and it is mostly through the trot that the horse will achieve self-carriage. The gradual improvement at the trot will also influence the work at the canter and at the walk.

The ordinary walk must show rhythm and energy, and it helps to count the footfalls steadily—one-two-three-four—as you ride round the arena. Make sure the horse is straight and practise riding on a circle, and turning and changing direction without any loss of rhythm or energy.

The Free Walk

In the free walk the horse must lengthen and stretch his neck and his hind hoofprints must be seen clearly to over-track those of the forelegs. The rein contact is very slight and the walk is unhurried. Go round the arena at an ordinary walk and change the rein across the diagonal from quarter marker to quarter marker at a free walk. Encourage the horse to lower and stretch his head and neck by allowing the reins to slip gently through your fingers until the rein becomes long and there is little contact. Let the hands move forward in time with the sway and movement of the walk. If he throws his head, say 'No', and with stronger contact, widen and lower your hands for an instant to explain to the horse what you want him to do. In more difficult cases, when the horse refuses to

The free walk on a long rein. The horse's head has turned to the right but he is striding forward well and overtracking his fore feet with his hind feet. The rider has lost the right rein momentarily. The left rein is correct for long rein when the horse's head is straight.

47

lower or stretch his head at all, it may help to allow him a mouthful of grass on his way across the diagonal. He soon appreciates this opportunity and will be only too ready to lower his head on the next attempt across the diagonal in the hope of more grass. You must not overdo this or you will have another problem to deal with, but it can be used with discretion as an explanation and as a means of persuading the horse to lower and stretch of his own accord and without any force or argument.

THE FREE WALK ON A LOOSE REIN

This is virtually the same except that there is no direct contact between the rider's hand and the horse's mouth other than through the weight of the reins. The horse is completely free to lower and stretch his head and neck as much as he likes. It affords him the opportunity to relax totally and to stretch and rest the muscles which have been in play. Use this free walk on a loose rein whenever the horse is learning a new lesson or at any time when he is tense or apprehensive. It will relax and reassure him and he will return to his work more able to cope with its demands.

The free walk on a loose rein. Contact is maintained by the weight of the reins.

THE TURN ON THE HAUNCHES

This is a preliminary to the High School movement of the pirouette at the canter. The Event horse is required to perform only a simple turn on the haunches to either rein and then the half pirouettes to left and right at the walk. His training up to first class Three-Day-Event standard dressage takes him to the start of High School work, and all the work he does in his preparation for this is laying a firm foundation for future advanced work. The approach to the turn on the haunches is as before; proceed in a line parallel to a well-defined fence and halt. This time, however, you remain on the

Left turn on the haunches. The off-fore crosses over the near fore. The horse's head and neck incline left.

track and not one metre away from it. Assuming you are on the left rein, the turn on the haunches will be to the left. The hind legs will form the pivot around which the forelegs will describe a 180° half circle. The forelegs move in regular steps with the off-fore crossing over and in front of the near-fore. The off-hind describes a small half circle round the near-hind which marks time on the spot.

In the perfect turn, the sequence of four-time footfall remains clear and each leg is lifted and returns to the ground as it would in the walk. The horse must not step backwards nor must he pivot on his hind legs with them rooted firmly to the ground. The aids are as follows: inside hand—to give flexion and direction; outside leg applied one hand behind the girth; the inside leg lies just behind the girth, maintaining forward impulsion so that the horse does not step backwards; the outside hand balances the degree of the turn.

In the first attempts, allow the horse to make only one step at a time until he understands what you want. Make much of him as soon as he does right, and continue to ask for another step until the turn is completed. Walk on, describe a half circle to change the rein, and return to the same place to try again. Continue this exercise until the horse is able to describe a full 180° turn to the left and then repeat it all on the other rein for the turn to the right. Keep the horse calm always, but if he becomes upset and it is clear he genuinely cannot work out what he is to do, stop the lesson immediately. Restore his confidence by working on something he enjoys and finds easy and then gently return to the turns. In a really bad case of confusion, you must stop the lesson altogether for the day and start again the following morning. It is your responsibility as trainer to decide whether the horse is being awkward and boorish and is simply refusing to co-operate or that he is genuinely confused and needs a clearer explanation and reassurance.

THE REIN BACK

The rein back is a two-time diagonal movement with the off-fore and near-hind forming one diagonal pair and the near-fore and off-hind the other. The steps back must be clear and definite and regular, and the horse must remain perfectly straight. The rider has to guard against the quarters escaping to one side or the other, and against resistances in the mouth and the back. The movement should be smooth and effortless with the head still and the mouth closed.

The rein back. A diagonal movement. The horse remains on the bit and steps back firmly and quietly.

Initially, walk the horse up to a fence. Halt one pace away from it. Keep the horse on the bit with combined effect: raise the hands slightly and vibrate the reins with your fingers; apply the legs on the girth with gentle vibrations. As soon as the horse relaxes his jaw and lowers his head, lower your hands to the normal correct position and take the legs to their place just behind the girth. The horse is at attention and ready for your next instruction. You want the horse to step back readily and on no account must you pull him back with strong tension on the bit. There must be no backward tension and the only difference between your aids to walk on and the aids to rein back is in the action of the hand, and the shifting of your weight. When you want the horse to walk on you close your legs behind the girth and open the hand. In the aids to rein back, you close your legs just behind the girth but the hand remains closed. You lean forward slightly. The horse starts to go forward but is prevented from doing so by the barrier of the hand. His immediate reaction is to take a step back. Reward him as soon as he does this and try again.

Do not remain at the fence all the time. Between your attempts walk away from it, circle, and return to halt in the same place. In this way, you encourage the horse to maintain the forward movement and he will be less inclined to go rigid in his back and become insensitive in his mouth. The horse is allowed to take one step forward before you close your hand if he appears not to understand at first that he is to step back. Sometimes this helps him to muster the impulsion necessary to rein back correctly. Practise quietly until he can manage three or four consecutive steps and use the voice as an additional aid with a clear 'COME BACK'.

He is ready now to repeat the lesson in the open, away from the fence barrier. If your arena is enclosed, the perimeter walls will provide support and guidance as the horse reins back from a halt parallel to the side. In this case remember to practise equally on both reins so that he is not relying continually for support on one side. He must learn to rein back with no supporting wall, and he should be taken into the middle of the arena to practise until he is able to manage six steps with pure diagonals and with neither resistance nor evasion.

The horse by now has graduated from the first stage of training. He has developed the propelling power of the hocks and pushes freely forward from behind. Conformation and temperament will dictate the length of time it takes to reach this stage, and the ideal is to allow six months for this early training to ensure perfect basic paces. Unfortunately, it is virtually impossible to spend this amount of time on the first stage, and the horse will be lucky if he has three months in which to develop the propelling power of the hocks.

The second stage is to gain self carriage and you will do this by driving and half halting so that the forehand is gradually raised and the quarters lowered. The centre of gravity will move back over the centre. His progress now will depend on conformation, temperament and aptitude to learn.

CHAPTER SEVEN
*Preliminary exercises as preparation for two track work.
Teaching the aids to the horse. Leg yielding. Riding in
position*

The horse should now learn the aids for work on two tracks.
Obviously he cannot be expected to absorb all the two track
movements in a series of consecutive lessons, and this chapter
contains the preliminary introduction of the aids and the explanation of them to the horse, and also the invaluable exercises of
'leg yielding' and 'riding in position'.

The work overall will take a considerable amount of time, and
you must continually bear in mind how very important it is to
avoid confusing the horse and that one lesson must be clearly
understood before the next is started. The work on four, three and
two tracks has tremendous advantages in that the horse will begin
to understand thoroughly 'going away from the leg'. The problem
of straightening him when his quarters have swung to either side
is subsequently solved. He will be very much more manoeuvrable
to open and shut gates, and his length bend will improve considerably and become second nature with the practice and per-
fecting of 'riding in position'. The horse will become infinitely
more supple.

The first lesson is to teach him the aids to go sideways, and you
start by walking him up to a fence and halting in front of it. You
are going to ask him for a full pass to the left, remembering that
the prime object is for him to learn the aids and that you are not
concerned at this stage with the regularity of the steps. The first
attempts are bound to be ragged and hesitant but all his efforts in
the right direction should be acknowledged with a pleased voice
and a pat on the neck. Once again, if he goes backwards or turns
round, the decisive '*No*' comes into effect and you walk away from
the fence and then return to the same place, facing it, for a second
attempt. The first indication to the horse for the full pass to the
left from the halt is to take your left hand out to the left with the
fingers vibrating gently. Prevent the horse from merely turning
left by balancing this with the controlling right hand. Apply your

right leg well behind the girth and say 'OVER' in a clear voice. If your aids are strong enough the horse will take the odd faltering step sideways and as soon as he has done this, halt, then reward him and relax a moment. Take one step forwards to achieve impulsion, turn right and walk first away from the fence and then back to it to try again. Repeat the performance several times until the horse can take three or four steady steps sideways. After halting, always turn right, away from the fence when teaching him the left full pass and left, after halting, when doing the right full pass; remember never to go away from the fence in a continuous movement after the sideways steps. You must finish the full pass with a halt, pat the horse, and then move forward and turn. In this way the horse will not be encouraged merely to turn left or right instead of stepping sideways. You make the two movements completely separately. When the horse has learned the aids to the left, ask him for the right full pass. Preface this by circling right, at the walk—with a diameter of about twelve metres—two or three times, before halting in front of the fence and applying the aids. The right hand moves out to the right, fingers vibrating gently, and the hand kept low. The left hand prevents the horse from turning right. The left leg is applied strongly well behind the girth, and remember to use the voice clearly—OVER. After two or three days the horse should be able to take a few steps both to the left and to the right. There will always be more difficulty with one side than the other and this will probably apply throughout the work on four, three and two tracks. You will have to practise more on the weaker side so that eventually the horse becomes equally adept on both reins.

When it is apparent that the horse clearly understands that he is to move sideways away from your leg, you can leave the fence and ask him for the same movement in the arena. Having completed the full pass and having halted as before, instead of turning as you did at the fence, ask the horse to move forward. This encourages the horse to resume immediately the forward movement he will have lost momentarily in the full pass. The restraining fence is no longer there and now you can make sure he is crossing his legs correctly and is not stepping backwards. He must cross his off-fore over and in front of the near-fore, and his off-hind over the near hind when going to the left; and his near-fore and near-hind over the off-fore and off-hind respectively when going to the right. It will be easier for the horse to do this if he is allowed to move forward obliquely so that the movement becomes a compromise between the full pass and the 45° angle of a half pass.

The next stage is to practise the oblique movement at the walk.

Take the left rein round the arena and, as you emerge from the second corner of the short side and approach the quarter marker, give a half halt and apply the aids. The left hand moves to the left giving the horse the correct bend in head and neck. The horse's left eye should be visible to the rider. The right hand controls the degree of the sideways movement but remains on the right side and does not cross the horse's withers. The right leg is applied one hand behind the girth and the left leg lies just behind the girth to ensure that impulsion and forward movement are maintained. It will be enough to ask the horse to move from the quarter marker to the centre line and as soon as you reach the centre line, allow the horse to straighten out. Continue up the centre line making sure that he is perfectly straight and at the top of the arena turn left. Circle once and repeat the movement until he can do it easily, maintaining regular footfalls and forward impulsion. Practise until he is equally good on both reins and can go from quarter marker to centre line, up the centre and turn—changing the rein—to the next quarter marker so that he is moving obliquely first from right to left at one quarter marker, and then from left to right at the next with no intervening circle. By this time, the horse has thoroughly understood the aids to go sideways.

The following exercises of leg yielding and riding in position are designed to teach the rider to 'feel' the horse and to be able to influence correctly the positioning of his head and neck and of his body. In leg yielding the horse learns to give to the rider's leg. In riding in position the horse learns to flex in his head and neck.

Leg Yielding

In this exercise the horse remains perfectly straight in his body but the head is turned slightly away from the direction of the movement. The horse moves on four tracks. Leg yielding teaches lateral aids—hand and leg on the same side. It will come easily to the horse if he has learned his first lesson well, for leg yielding is simply 'giving' to the rider's leg. He has already been taught to go away from the leg at the walk. The following movements of leg yielding and riding in position are practised always at the sitting trot. They prepare the horse for perfect length bend in corners, circles and turns and also for the more demanding movements of 'shoulder-in', 'travers' (head to the wall), 'renvers' (tail to the wall), and to the ultimate half pass with counter change of hand. The preliminary explanation of the aids as practised already against the fence and in the arena will be a considerable help in these more generally accepted exercises.

Leg Yielding to the Outside Leg: The exercise is on four tracks. Begin

Leg yielding to the outside leg. The four tracks can clearly be seen: off-fore, off-hind, near-fore, near-hind.

to trot round the arena on the left rein, sitting, and at the first quarter marker on the long side, apply the right leg one hand behind the girth: the left leg lies just behind the girth. The horse's quarters move half a step on to the inside track. He remains straight except for his head which is turned very slightly right—away from the direction in which he is moving. The right hand maintains strong contact and the left dictates only the degree of bend allowed in the head and neck. Before the next quarter marker, straighten the horse back on to the track. In this particular instance, you straighten the horse by adjusting the quarters to the forehand. Make sure you ride through the approaching corner correctly with even length bend and a perfect arc.

Leg Yielding to the Inside Leg: The exercise is on four tracks. This movement is exactly the same in principle as the preceding one except that the horse yields to the rider's inside leg. The quarters move fractionally off the track towards the outside as the inside leg is applied; the horse remains in a straight line through his body, but his head and neck are bent slightly away from the direction in which he is moving. Trot round the arena on the left rein, sitting trot, and at the quarter marker—when the horse is absolutely straight—apply the inside leg one hand behind the girth. The horse's quarters move fractionally away from the track towards the outside. The inside hand flexes the horse very slightly away from the direction in which he is moving. The outside hand controls the degree of the flexion. Hold this position and proceed along the long side of the arena. Do not ask for too great an angle. The movement is on four tracks only. When the horse is on four

Leg yielding to the inside leg. The horse is on four tracks: off-hind, off-fore, near-hind, near-fore.

tracks one hind leg moves to a position between the two forelegs and the other hind leg of necessity completes the fourth track outside the forelegs. Practise the exercise equally on both reins.

The final exercise is to leg yield first to the outside and then to the inside from quarter marker to quarter marker, remembering to straighten the horse positively and clearly for one or two strides at the centre marker. As always, the exercise must be practised until the horse is equally proficient on both reins.

RIDING IN POSITION

This exercise is preparatory to 'shoulder-in'. In inside position, the horse learns the use of the inside rein and is prepared for perfect length bend. In outside position the horse learns the use of the outside rein. The movement is almost on four tracks by virtue of the positioning of head and neck. One hind leg moves slightly from its normal position of being in a straight line with the corresponding foreleg to a position between the two forelegs, the other hind leg moves of necessity to an equidistant position outside the other three legs.

Inside Position: Take the right rein. Begin as usual by trotting around the arena and prepare to ride in inside position on the long side. The horse should be bent in his head and neck only—his body remains straight—and the flexion is as if he were on the right circle. At the quarter marker make sure the horse is straight. Feel the inside rein and carry it slightly to the inside to give the horse inside flexion. The outside hand opens to allow the necessary degree of bend in head and neck. The inside leg maintains the

Riding in inside position. The horse is bent in head and neck and instead of being completely straight he tends to move almost on four tracks. The bend is in head and neck only.

forward movement. You should be conscious of the horse's inside eye, his right one when he is on the right rein. Progress up the long side of the arena with head and neck flexed as if you were on a right circle and then straighten out the horse preparatory to riding through the corner. Repeat the exercise down the next long side, using the length bend coming round the corner as a guide and positioning the horse's head and neck as already described before moving down the long side of the arena. Riding in inside position is the preparatory exercise for perfect length bend in all corners, turns and circles, and for shoulder-in and travers (head to the wall). In inside position, on the right rein, the horse is held as if he were moving on to a right circle. In inside position on the left rein, the horse is held as if he were moving on to the left circle.

You must realise that in all these exercises the horse is not required to show much bend in his head and neck, and with one hind leg placed between the two forelegs and the remaining hind leg placed equidistantly one side or other of the forelegs, he is not yet approaching the angle demanded in work on two or even three tracks. This will come later in the more advanced exercises of travers and renvers (two tracks), and shoulder-in (three tracks) respectively.

Outside Position: The aids are the same as those for riding in inside position but in this case, riding on the right rein, the horse must show left flexion in his head and neck—as if he were commencing a circle left. Riding on the left rein, the horse shows right flexion— as if he were moving on to a right circle. Take the right rein, sitting trot, and ride carefully through the corner. Make sure that the horse is absolutely straight before the quarter marker on the long side of the arena. Feel the left rein to achieve flexion to the

Riding in outside position. Again the horse is bent in head and neck only and instead of being completely straight he tends to move on four tracks.

left in head and neck only. Control the degree of flexion with the right rein. Apply the left leg behind the girth to maintain the rhythm and forward movement, and proceed along the side of the arena in this position as if the horse were circling left. Straighten out the horse at the quarter marker before the corner.

When the horse is able to maintain inside position up one side of the arena and outside position down the other side, you can practise a combination of the two. From quarter marker to quarter marker start first with inside position and change to outside position at the half way marker. Go from one position to the other without straightening the horse. This exercise is used to get the horse in hand and to prepare him for smaller circles and turns. The hind leg on the inside of the curve has to work well under the horse.

CHAPTER EIGHT

The basic paces achieved. Increase and decrease at the trot

The horse is now capable of good basic paces at the ordinary walk, trot and canter. He can describe a circle showing the correct bend to the inside, and is able to turn and corner so that the whole length of his body from head to quarters follows a perfect arc or circle—length bend. He should never be more bent in his head and neck than he is behind, as this causes the quarters to swing and could even injure the horse. Perfect length bend is described when the horse is bent evenly around the rider's inside leg. It is required in every corner, turn, circle or change of direction and later on in the work on two tracks.

Increase at the trot — the lengthened strides. The outline is still long, the horse has not yet gained self carriage.

The horse also understands clearly our aids for the progressive transitions from halt to canter and can work without losing his balance in an arena 60 × 30 yards. He will go away from the leg and can be straightened easily. He is now ready to learn the increase and decrease of paces preparatory to extension and collection. As before, you start with the trot and proceed around the arena at an ordinary but active pace. Emerging from the corner on the long side, give the horse a half halt to call him to attention and, making sure he is absolutely straight, close both legs on the girth and allow your weight to shift very slightly

Decrease at the trot — the shortened strides. The horse momentarily achieves self carriage, his centre of gravity moves back and the forehand lightens.

backwards. The fractional movement of weight pushes the horse's hind legs further under him and drives him forward from behind. At the same time, use the voice as an additional aid, T-ROT ON. Open the hands slightly to allow the horse's head and neck to stretch forward whilst still maintaining steady contact, and close them as soon as the horse has given a few lengthened strides. You want the horse to show a marked difference in his trot by using his hind legs more actively and further underneath him. His hocks must be well bent and supple and not trail behind him, and his outline must lengthen a little as his stride lengthens. Ask him for only a few strides at first and make much of him as soon as he lengthens his stride with impulsion.

The horse's back at this stage may give the first indications of beginning to 'swing', another of our ultimate aims. It takes time for the horse to learn to use his back and to relax in his work, and once his spine becomes less rigid the rider will be able to sit more easily and more comfortably and will not be 'thrown' to anything like the same extent. The main reaction to the first attempt at lengthening the stride is for the horse to 'run', taking faster and faster strides. He must be restrained immediately, settled back into an ordinary trot as before and asked again at the same quarter marker emerging from the corner. In this way, you explain to the horse that that is not what is wanted, and you return to the place where you first asked for the longer strides. This will instil upon him that whenever he makes a mistake you will ask again quietly but determinedly until he produces the right answer.

Persevere in asking for a few lengthened strides until the horse goes forward immediately into more active and longer strides and has obviously realised what is wanted. Then ask him to maintain the increase until he is able to go from one quarter marker to the next on the long side of the arena. Ask him only for an increase on the long sides or when changing the rein across the diagonal and, as always, work equally on both reins to prevent the horse from becoming one-sided.

Next, he must learn to decrease the pace and, starting again at the ordinary trot, ask for an increase and lengthening of the stride from quarter marker to half way marker. At the half way marker close both hands, apply both legs quietly on the girth—at the same time making sure the back is strong and straight and that the seat bones are pressing well down into the saddle. The horse immediately closes up between the barrier of hand and leg and reverts to an ordinary trot. A half halt and once again apply the same aids. This time, however, you will need stronger leg aids to create greater impulsion. The hind legs are driven further under the horse, the hand prevents him from going forward faster. He lowers his quarters a little, raises his forehand and achieves, if only momentarily, the start of a more collected trot. The actual decrease you are after at this stage does not approach the extent of true collection but it is important to continue to drive the horse forward when the hand has stopped him for an instant and slowed his pace.

The impulsion and free forward movement must be maintained and the whole procedure is as if you were opening and closing the throttle of a car. The collective paces are a veritable store of energy. Having explained the lesson, practise and practise until the horse increases and decreases his trot on demand. He will become progressively lighter in hand and more responsive, and if you begin to sit to the trot whenever you ask for a decrease of pace the horse will associate this with a more collected, active and energetic

Activating the inside hind leg by describing a small circle. The horse is encouraged towards the second stage of training, self carriage. In this picture the hind leg is engaged well under the horse but he is a little too bent in inside flexion with his head and neck.

trot and begin to offer it of his own accord whenever you sit in the saddle. Make full use of all the school figures at the ordinary and decreased paces of the trot and encourage the horse towards the second stage of training, self carriage, by describing smaller and smaller circles. This has the effect of immediately activating the hind leg and bringing it further under the horse. The forehand is consequently raised and the centre of gravity inevitably shifts further backwards from the forehand.

If the horse persists in running instead of lengthening his stride across the diagonal, it is time to check on your own riding position. Make sure your leg aids are applied with equal pressure on either side of the horse and in absolutely the same place. The hands must have equal contact and be very steady. The back must be strong and straight and the seat bones pressing well down in the saddle.

Having made sure of all this, we start again at an ordinary trot round the arena, describe a twenty metre circle at one end and begin to ask the horse for a decrease in pace. First a half halt, then gradual but strong driving leg aids and firm and steady contact with the hands. The horse closes up like a concertina so that his outline is shortened and his stride more energetic. Ask him for a ten metre circle in the corner of the arena preparatory to emerging from the small circle and straightening out to change the rein across the diagonal. The procedure, therefore, is as follows: (1) half halt; (2) transition from ordinary trot to shortened, very active trot on top twenty metre circle; (3) short active trot on ten metre circle in corner of the arena; (4) straighten horse out of circle and change rein across the diagonal from quarter marker to quarter marker. As the horse moves from the quarter marker across the arena maintain firm and steady contact with the reins, lowering and widening them momentarily to ensure that the horse is straight. Then push him forwards using the legs with equal pressure just behind the girth and forcing the seat bones hard down into the saddle before assuming rising trot. The horse should immediately lengthen his stride with true impulsion from behind. Allow him only a few strides of extension or increase and bring him back to an ordinary trot well before the approaching quarter marker.

At the end of this lesson the horse should be very much more responsive to the legs, lighter in hand and softer in his back. You are laying the foundations of perfect self carriage.

CHAPTER NINE
Increase and decrease at the canter

The same rules apply as you work on the canter increase and decrease. The aim of the exercise once again is to make the horse more responsive to the leg and to make him lighter in hand as his hind leg moves further under him and his impulsion increases. First trot round the arena and then go on the circle at either end. Describe a perfect circle, give the horse a half halt and make a smooth transition to canter with the inside foreleg leading. It may help in the early stages to describe a larger circle of approximately twenty-five metres, as some horses, particularly the bigger ones, may be thrown off balance with the increase of pace and become disunited. Should this happen, bring the horse back to an ordinary trot at once, make sure he is straight on the circle with good length bend, and again give the aid to canter.

Having established a good canter on the circle, ask the horse for an increase of pace. Apply both legs behind the girth and open the hands fractionally to allow the horse to lengthen his stride. Encourage him to lengthen his neck as well as his outline by 'giving' with the outside rein in just the same way as you would to bring him on the inside rein. The outside hand goes forward and back in a smooth one-two movement over the space of two full strides. Guard against the common fault of carrying the inside hand across the withers to the outside. This is unfortunately a natural reaction of the rider when the horse begins to fall in on the circle. The correct answer in fact is to take the inside hand towards the centre of the circle, maintaining steady contact and thereby giving the horse a clear indication for the inside bend. The outside hand balances this action outwards by holding the horse on a correct circle and dictating the required size of the circle. The inside leg fractionally behind the girth, keeps the horse out on the circle and the outside leg one hand behind the girth, stops the quarters from swinging to the outside and bends the horse round the inside leg. The weight, as always at the canter on the circle, is on the inside seat bone, and the rider's outside shoulder is slightly forward so that his shoulders are parallel with those of the horse.

The horse is asked to increase the pace on the circle and to lengthen his stride. Just as in the trot you want a lengthening of the stride and not a quickening of the pace, allow the horse to increase for a full circle and then, closing both legs on the girth and closing the hands, return to an ordinary canter. Continue to do this until the horse understands what is wanted and will increase his pace smoothly and steadily. There must be no throwing of the head or rushing forwards and if the first attempts are restricted to work on the circle the horse will make no attempt to rush off or to become in any way excited. He must be kept calm and unruffled throughout the lesson and it is important to allow him to relax frequently by making the transitions down to a walk and, after a few strides of an energetic ordinary walk, by giving the horse a loose rein and encouraging him to relax for a minute or two.

The next attempt takes place on the circle at the other end of the arena, remaining on the same rein to eliminate any possibility

Increase at the canter on the long side of the arena. The outline is long, the horse goes freely forward with a long stride. Compare this with the extended canter on page 77.

Decrease at the canter. The centre of gravity has moved backwards and the forehand is lightened. The strides become shorter and more rounded. Compare this with the collected canter on page 77.

of confusion. Ask for an increase of pace once round the circle, close hands and legs and return to an ordinary canter. Then close both legs again to drive the hind legs further under the horse and, instead of 'giving' with the hands which would result in an increase of pace, close the hands. The created impulsion is thus unable to escape forwards. It returns to the hind quarters which immediately lower: the centre of gravity moves backwards, and the forehand is raised. The rider continues to use his legs with firm and steady pressure to maintain the horse in canter, and, as the energy is controlled between, first, the legs which create the energy and, second, the hands which prevent it from escaping forward, the stride must become shorter and more rounded.

Having achieved the decrease in pace for a few strides only, open the hands fractionally and allow the horse to go forward into an ordinary canter. This exercise of increase and decrease is practised until the horse can increase and decrease his canter in immediate response to the rider's aids. The transition down is always the more difficult and it is essential that the rider's influence is correct and precise. Any loss of contact, however momentary, will result in the horse coming off the bit and considerable concentration must be applied to ensure absolutely equal pressure of both legs in the transition. If the legs are applied unevenly the horse's quarters will swing either to the outside or to the inside. The outside leg must be applied more strongly if the quarters swing outwards, and if the quarters swing inwards the inside leg is used to push the quarters outwards and straighten the horse.

With constant practise the horse becomes adept at these transitions and once he produces them accurately and calmly on the circle, the rider can ask for the increase on the long side of the arena. Once again he must make sure that the work is practised equally on both reins. If the horse is weaker on one side it will be necessary to concentrate on that side until the weakness is eliminated and the horse is equally happy on either rein. It is of paramount importance that the horse remains straight in the increase or decrease of pace and in the transitions.

c

Work on two tracks at the trot. Shoulder-in: travers: renvers: half pass and counter change of hand on two tracks

Two track work is done on two tracks as the name implies. The angle between the tracks is 45° or one step difference. The work makes the horse obedient to the aids and teaches the rider co-ordination and feeling. It becomes imperative to appreciate and to feel the angle at which the horse is bent and to be able to influence and control exactly the depth of the angle at which the horse is held. The rider must not give the horse too much bend in head and neck as this results in loss of rhythm and cadence. The work increases the suppleness and handiness of the horse and greatly advances his education.

SHOULDER-IN

Shoulder-in is one of the gymnastic exercises preparatory to the actual work on two tracks. In shoulder-in the horse moves on three tracks with great emphasis on length bend but the horse is bent away from the direction in which he is moving. Practised correctly it furthers the degree of collection, for the inside hind leg has to

Shoulder-in on the right rein. The movement is shown clearly to be on three tracks. The horse is bent away from the direction in which he is moving.

push under the horse and carry the weight of both horse and rider. The rider gains complete domination of the quarters.

Start the lesson by practising riding in inside position, which is the exercise preparatory to shoulder-in. This is to make the horse understand more clearly what we want him to do. Take the right rein and trot round the arena having the horse active and compliant. Describe a ten metre circle at the bottom end of the arena, in sitting trot, and move down the long side of the arena in inside position. Repeat this two or three times and then prepare to ask for shoulder-in along the next long side. Remain in sitting trot throughout this preparation and for the ensuing lesson. Describe a ten metre circle again in the top corner of the arena, still on the right rein and, having completed the circle by returning to the first quarter marker on the long side, allow the horse to move half a step with his forehand to the inside and maintain the right length bend. In this position, begin to move obliquely left up towards the next quarter marker, retaining the right length bend throughout the movement.

Your aids are as follows: inside rein to give flexion right; inside leg one hand behind the girth. The outside rein and outside leg confirm and maintain the horse's length bend and prevent shoulder and quarters from escaping outwards. The horse is bent longitudinally as if he were on a right circle. The off-fore is half a step off the track to the inside, the near-fore and off-hind are on the track in a straight line, the near-hind is half a step off the track to the outside. The horse is bent away from the direction in which he is moving.

The inside hind leg initiates the movement of shoulder-in and at first the horse will find it difficult to sustain the increased effort which this position demands. The hock has to develop increased flexion and must tread sideways under the body to a considerable extent so that it can carry the weight. The horse will be inclined to try to evade the movement and will lose his rhythm and impulsion. When this happens, you simply retake the circle and start again. Returning to the circle allows the hock action and rhythm to be re-established and no further attempt should be made until the horse has recovered his activity.

Ask the horse for shoulder-in from the quarter marker as you emerge from the introductory circle, up to the centre marker. This is enough for the early lessons. At the centre marker move forward again on to a ten metre circle to re-establish the hock action and, having completed the circle, go straight on round the arena. Repeat the exercise down the next long side. Circle in the corner, shoulder-in from quarter marker to half way marker, circle again

67

and straight on. Increase the duration of the shoulder-in as the horse becomes more accustomed to it until you are able to move from quarter marker to quarter marker. Straighten the horse at the quarter marker and ride through the corners correctly.

Practise shoulder-in equally on both reins until the horse finds it no problem and can maintain his rhythm and impulsion throughout the movement. This exercise is also an invaluable aid against shying. The natural reaction when a horse shies away from an object is to try to persuade him to face up to it. You can save yourself a great deal of time and effort by immediately placing the horse in shoulder-in position, head away from the intimidating object. Your aids in this position are so strong that it is almost impossible for him to take any further notice of what is frightening him, and you will be past it before he realises what has happened.

TRAVERS

Travers, or Head to the Wall, is the first exercise the horse is taught where he moves approximately on two tracks. It improves the length bend of the horse and his suppleness, and completely confirms his correct bend through the corners and turns. It is the second of the gymnastic exercises.

Once again your first attempt is made from a circle. Taking the right rein, sitting trot, describe a ten metre circle at the bottom of the arena. In this case the circle starts in the corner of the arena. Concentrate on the length bend on the circle. Check that the horse is flexed to the inside and you can just glimpse his right eye. Feel the continual bend throughout his body around your inside leg. Keep the horse on a true circle with your outside rein and leg. On completing the circle give a half halt and, instead of straightening the horse to go up the long side of the arena, continue to hold the

Travers or 'Head to the Wall'. The horse is on the left rein and is clearly on two tracks sideways. He looks in the direction in which he is moving.

horse in the length bend position. This exercise differs from shoulder-in in that the horse looks in the direction in which he is moving. Despite the fact that length bend is maintained in all three of the gymnastic exercises of shoulder-in, travers and renvers, each exercise is completely different by reason of the position where the movement is started. Travers, or head to the wall, requires that the horse, on the right rein, maintains length bend to the right whilst he progresses to the right on two tracks. The moment the movement starts is the moment when the horse's head reaches the track on the long side of the arena. This means the aids for travers must be applied as the horse is rounding the corner at the bottom of the arena. Give the horse inside flexion with the inside rein; the inside leg lies just behind the girth; the outside leg is applied one hand further back. The horse moves sideways, his forelegs forming one track and his hindlegs the second track. His outside foreleg crosses over and in front of the inside foreleg. The outside hind leg crosses over and in front of the inside hind leg.

RENVERS

Renvers, or Tail to the Wall, is the third and last of the gymnastic exercises. Like travers, it improves the horse's length bend and suppleness and confirms his correct bend through corners and turns. Again, the horse moves on approximately two tracks.

The horse, on the right rein, is bent longitudinally as if he were on a left circle, and on the left rein he shows right length bend. The introductory circle, therefore, is not applicable.

Take the right rein and, at the quarter marker on the long side of the arena, position your horse in left length bend. The outside rein gives flexion to the left; the outside leg lies just behind the girth; the inside leg is applied one hand behind the girth; the

Renvers or 'Tail to the Wall'. The horse is on the left rein and is on two tracks sideways. He is bent as if he were on a right circle.

69

horse moves on two tracks from right to left along the long side of the arena, looking in the direction in which he is moving. His forelegs form one approximate track, his hindlegs the second. His off-fore crosses over and in front of the near-fore. His off-hind crosses over and in front of the near-hind. Straighten the horse at the second quarter marker before riding through the corners.

These exercises advance the rider's domination over the horse and increase his ability to place and to control the forehand and quarters to a required degree. The horse learns to use his hind legs with greater flexion and stronger delivery and his back becomes more supple. He is infinitely more handy and better balanced.

HALF PASS

In the half pass, the horse moves on two tracks with a very slight bend in the direction in which he is moving. The forehand—head, neck and shoulders—is slightly in advance of the quarters. The outside foreleg must cross over and in front of the inside foreleg and the outside hind leg crosses over and in front of the inside hind leg. The movement activates the shoulder.

Position the horse as follows to obtain a half pass: (i) make sure the horse is straight; (ii) give head and neck position; (iii) give slight length bend; and (iv) go into the movement with forehand leading slightly.

Take the left rein and go from the quarter marker to the centre line at the half pass. In order to do this, emerge from the corner at the bottom of the arena on to the long side and make sure the horse is straight. Feel the inside rein, taking it slightly towards the inside. This gives the horse inside flexion and his head looks to the left. The inside leg is just behind the girth; the outside leg is applied one hand further back. Your weight goes into and with the movement and is on the inside seat bone. The horse moves at a 45° angle and your shoulders and seat bones must adjust so that you remain parallel to the horse's shoulders and are going with the movement. Use the inside leg to maintain the forward movement and the impulsion. Arriving at the centre line, straighten the horse, proceed up to the top end of the arena, turn left and repeat the exercise.

Once the horse has understood the lesson on both reins, alternate left half pass with right half pass. Start on the left rein, go from quarter marker to centre line in left half pass, proceed up the centre line and turn right at the top end of the arena. At the quarter marker go to the centre line in right half pass and proceed down the centre line to the bottom end of the arena. The horse arrives on the centre line with the forehand leading the quarters only

Make sure the horse is straight as he emerges from the corner.

Give head and neck position and slight length bend.

Into the movement on two tracks. The forehand leads slightly.

Approaching X.

Straight at X.

The new bend from X, and away into the right half pass.

fractionally. It is only too easy to allow the quarters to lead the forehand and this is a bad fault. You must position the horse clearly at the start of the movement and feel and maintain the angle throughout it. You must concentrate also on maintaining the impulsion. There should be no difference in the beat of the footfalls in the transitions from trotting round the arena and moving across it in half pass. Count or sing to yourself in time with the beat of the trot and do not alter the rhythm as you move into half pass.

COUNTER CHANGE OF HAND ON TWO TRACKS

This movement is included in the Three-Day-Event test. The horse is required to move on two tracks from the quarter marker to the centre X and away from X to the next quarter marker. First the horse moves one way on two tracks and then returns on the other rein on two tracks.

The greatest difficulty arising from this movement is in the change of bend and direction at the centre X. The horse must show a perfect half pass from the first quarter marker to X, his forehand slightly in advance of his quarters. He must then show clearly the change to the opposite half pass.

Take the left rein and move from the quarter marker towards the centre X on two tracks. Instead of aiming exactly for X, take a line which will bring you to the centre line several strides before X. As you approach the line straighten out the horse. Allow him to proceed on the centre line and, as you approach X, feel the right rein, position the horse for the half pass to the right and move on two tracks to the next quarter marker.

Practise this until you are sure you can straighten the horse and position him correctly for the return on two tracks. In this way you will be able to effect the change of bend clearly, without the danger of going into the second half pass with the quarters leading. Repeat the lesson, starting on the right rein.

The horse learns quickly and you must guard against possible anticipation by varying your demands at the half pass. Do not always ask for a counter change of hand once you have reached this standard. Insist that the horse goes straight up the centre line just as often as he returns on a counter change of hand. The temptation for the horse to anticipate will be greatly reduced and he will learn to wait for your aids.

The work on four, three and two tracks may be summarised to clarify the degree of bend required as follows:

1. Leg Yielding—the horse is straight. Four tracks.
2. Shoulder-In—has the greatest degree of bend. Three tracks.
3. Travers and Renvers—have the next greatest amount of length bend. Two tracks.
4. Half Pass—has a very slight length bend. Two tracks.

CHAPTER ELEVEN

Collected and extended work at the walk, trot and canter. Half pirouettes

The horse is now well advanced into the second stage of training and has gained considerable self carriage. He accepts the bit happily in all his work. The hind legs are placed correctly under him and the forehand is raised so that the centre of gravity is over the centre of the horse. The neck is bent at the poll and the jaw is relaxed. He is completely straight, immediately responsive to the leg and shows marked rhythm in all his paces. As the horse moves towards the third stage of training, and begins to develop the carrying capacity of the hocks, his rhythm will intensify until it becomes cadence. Cadence is rhythm intensified and it cannot be achieved until the horse shows absolute impulsion coupled with absolute lightness.

COLLECTED AND EXTENDED PACES

The horse has already been taught the increase and decrease at the trot and the canter but these do not demand the same degree of energy and impulsion as the collected and extended paces. The collected paces show proper rhythm with maximum impulsion, the hocks are engaged well under the horse and the forehand consequently is raised. The impulsion goes upwards, not forwards, and the steps become elevated and shorter. The head approaches the vertical in all collected paces but must never be behind it which is a grave fault. When the head is behind the vertical the horse is overbent and tends to go on his forehand and instead of being bent at the poll he is bent at the third vertebra. His steps in the collected paces are shorter but more elevated and rounded and he becomes lighter and more mobile. His outline closes up and is compressed.

The extended paces show the same amount of energy and impulsion but the driving forces are released so that the horse increases his stride with frank power. The stride lengthens to cover as much ground as possible. The hind legs move well under

73

the horse with increased flexion of the hocks and the neck is extended. The outline lengthens.

THE COLLECTED TROT AND EXTENDED TROT

The collected trot is always performed sitting. You are much closer to the horse at a sitting rather than a rising trot, and will find it easier to become more conscious of the rhythm and to feel the swing of the movement. The horse's back at this stage should be supple and give a distinct impression of swinging. No longer should the horse 'throw' you out of the saddle as he did in the early stages of training. His back should form a comfortable cushion to the movement and, in time, the extended trot will be just as comfortable as the collected pace.

The extended trot. The horse moves in self carriage. The centre of gravity has shifted backwards and the forehand is light. The horse extends with the hindlegs well engaged and with impulsion. Compare this picture with the next one of an advanced horse's extension.

Your first attempt at true collection and extension starts with the extended pace. Proceed round the arena at an ordinary trot and prepare to change the rein across the diagonal from quarter marker to quarter marker. After the quarter marker, make sure the horse is straight, give a half halt, and allow your lower legs to move forward on to the girth. This action results in your weight moving back slightly and your seat bones press down into the saddle. The horse's quarters are pushed further underneath him. You must create the energy and impulsion, driving the horse forward from behind. If your fingers open too much, the horse will dive on to his forehand and begin to run, his strides becoming fast rather than long. You must feel the necessary degree for opening the hand and co-ordinate the action of legs, weight and hands so that the energy is created and maintained. Feel the power you create as it develops a longer stride, close the hand to bring the horse back to one or two strides of the ordinary trot, and try again immediately. Hold and

This horse has achieved the third stage of training, the carrying capacity of the hocks. He is much more able now to use himself to the utmost of his physical capabilities.

drive all the way across the arena. Close the hand on reaching the quarter marker and allow the legs to return to their normal position. You can ask for an extension also on the long sides of the arena, but remember never to ask for too much too soon. Allow the horse to increase the number of extended strides very gradually.

Make the transition back to an ordinary trot from the extension, and then continue to drive. This time do not allow the horse to increase his stride. Your hands form a barrier to prevent the energy from being released and consequently that energy has to bounce back to the quarters. The quarters lower, the forehand is raised and the stride becomes shorter and rounder. The horse becomes collected. His outline closes up like a concertina. Describe a small circle to activate the inside hind leg and to encourage it to tread even further under the body and then allow the horse to move forward into an ordinary trot. His outline immediately becomes

The collected trot. The horse is in self carriage and the trot is active and very regular. Compare this picture with the next one of the collected trot of an advanced horse.

75

The advanced horse at the collected trot. He is obviously perfectly balanced and moves lightly and freely in perfect cadence.

longer but he remains on the bit, in perfect balance, and still with energy and impulsion. You must take care not to be too sudden with your aids or to upset the horse in any way. Once the horse understands what is required, you can go direct from an extended trot to a collected trot and continue in the collected pace whilst describing small circles, half circles to change the rein and changes of direction. Increase the duration of the collected pace very gradually.

The aim is for the horse to move into an extended or collected pace with lightness and ease, demonstrating the perfect harmony and understanding which exists between horse and rider. As in all the previous lessons, do not ask for too much extension or too much collection at one time. It is a very gradual process and calls for a great deal of tact and patience. Good collection and extension are the result of careful and painstaking early work. Allow the horse to understand thoroughly what is wanted and increase the number of strides only in ratio to the horse's growing capabilities.

THE EXTENDED AND COLLECTED CANTER.

The same lesson is repeated at the canter except that your extensions take place on the long sides of the arena, and never across the diagonal. Take the right rein at the ordinary canter and prepare to ask for an extended canter from the quarter marker towards the next quarter marker. Make sure the horse is straight and then drive forward, allowing your back to become strong and your seat bones to push down into the saddle. Allow the horse to lengthen his neck slightly and to go forwards clearly and decisively. He must not rush but should extend quietly and calmly. Prevent any excitement by asking only for a few strides at first and then closing your legs just behind the girth, closing your hands and vibrating the inside rein.

The extended canter. The neck lengthens slightly and the horse moves forward with a lengthened stride and frank impulsion.

The collected canter. The outline is shorter, the centre of gravity back with the quarters correspondingly lowered and the forehand raised.

This action of the inside rein, especially in the transition down to an ordinary or collected canter at the quarter marker, is extremely important. It helps to emphasise to the horse that he must remain cantering with the inside foreleg leading, for it is very easy for him in this transition to lose his balance. A slight shifting of your weight or a little resistance and he will change behind and become disunited. Should this happen you stop the horse immediately by returning to the trot. Circle once to the inside, make a transition to canter and circle again. Ask for an extension from the quarter marker along the long side of the arena but this time begin to turn well before the next quarter marker, at the same time closing your hands and your legs and vibrating the inside rein. The horse will find it easier to remain cantering with the inside fore-leg leading if he is already on a gentle curve to the inside. Circle at the ordinary canter to regain or to consolidate the perfect three-time pace and then ask the horse for a collected canter.

Close your hands slightly, close your legs so that you create the energy and then restrain it. The energy returns to the hindquarters and the horse assumes the more advanced outline of shortened length, lowered quarters and raised forehand. His canter shortens, the action becomes more rounded, the energy and impulsion are even more apparent. Rhythm is intensified and becomes cadence. The three-time beat is very marked.

The horse will lapse into a four-time beat only if you ask for the collected pace at too early a stage in his training. If he has worked slowly and systematically through the programme he will be capable of a perfect collected canter almost at once. You must remember, as always, that it does not pay to rush the training and you will gain nothing but trouble if you try to push the horse too quickly. If he lapses into four-time, he is not ready for collection. You must continue to work on his ordinary canter, sending him forward energetically, and making use of the circles to stimulate the action of the inside hind leg and to encourage him to use it further under his body.

COLLECTED AND EXTENDED WALK

The collected walk is a vigorous and energetic pace, the steps shorter than in the ordinary walk but more rounded with the

The extended walk. The horse moves frankly forward with a lengthened stride and a longer neck.

The collected walk. The stride is shorter and more rounded. The walk is in strongly marked four time.

joints flexing markedly. The horse moves resolutely forward with head and neck raised. The head approaches the vertical position. The hind legs are engaged well under the horse.

The extended walk is a walk with a longer stride and in longer outline. Contact is maintained but the horse stretches out his head and neck a little with the head in front of the vertical. The horse covers as much ground as possible with each step but must maintain the regularity of the pace and his hind feet must touch the ground clearly beyond the prints of his forefeet.

Start the lesson with an ordinary walk and prepare to change the rein across the diagonal at an extended walk. Use your legs to push the horse forwards just before his hind legs leave the ground. Count the one-two-three-four of the walk sequence: near-hind, near-fore, off-hind, off-fore, until you are sure of the exact moment at which each hind leg leaves the ground. Maintain a steady but light contact and allow the horse to stretch his head and neck slightly. Your hands and arms move forwards and backwards in time with the movement. The horse lengthens his stride, his hind legs tread well under him and over-track the prints of his forefeet by as much as six inches with a free-striding and active horse.

The transition to a collected walk is obtained in just the same way as the other paces. Close your hands and continue to drive the horse up to his bit. The steps become shorter. The driving force of energy you are creating cannot escape forwards so the horse accentuates the flexion of his joints and the action becomes more rounded. Make sure the regularity of steps is maintained and the walk sequence is clearly defined. The collected walk is the pace from which you ask the horse for the first non-progressive transition to canter. Before that, he learns the half pirouette at the walk.

HALF PIROUETTE AT THE WALK

This exercise is a development of the turn on the haunches. The forehand describes a half circle around the hind legs and the inside hind leg forms the pivot. In the turn on the haunches the horse halts before attempting the turn, but in the half pirouette he is required to go into the movement, without a pause, from the very moment the inside hind leg stops going forward. The four-time beat continues throughout the turn and the inside hind leg marks time on the spot and must not become immobile.

The moment to ask for the half pirouette is when the inside hind leg is moving forward. Give the horse a half halt, take the inside rein slightly to the inside. Continue to drive forwards in order to maintain the impulsion and to keep the legs marching. Control the depth of the turn carefully so that the horse is turning only in his own length and is not stepping sideways, and apply more outside leg as the turn progresses. One step before it is completed, begin to straighten the horse and allow him to move forwards. Count out the walk sequence before the turn and continue to count as you turn and move away. The horse must turn smoothly, with even strides, crossing the outside foreleg over the inside foreleg, and with the outside hind leg describing a tiny half circle round the pivot, the inside hind leg. He must not be allowed to move backwards at any time in the movement.

CHAPTER TWELVE

Walk to canter transitions. Counter canter. Halt to canter transitions. Bloquer. Simple change of leg

WALK TO CANTER TRANSITIONS

The walk to canter transition is your next consideration. This should be absolutely no problem for by now the horse is obedient, he fully understands the aids, and is light in hand. Walk round the arena and describe a ten metre circle in the corner. Allow the walk to start at an ordinary pace and then make the transition to a collected walk. Do not ask for the canter until the collected walk is well established, and the horse is calm and confident. Completing the ten metre circle, give a half halt, raise the inside hand slightly and vibrate the fingers. Your weight moves on to the inside seat bone so your inside leg is applied just behind the girth. The weight on the inside and the vibrations of the raised inside rein are already recognised by the horse and he strikes off automatically into the canter with the inside foreleg leading. As soon as he does this, make much of him and then concentrate on a good ordinary canter.

The transition down is more difficult and you must guard against the horse falling on to his forehand and losing his balance. The transition must be direct, from canter to walk, with no trot strides. The three-time of the canter merges smoothly into the walk from the third footfall. On the right rein, the canter sequence is as follows: near-hind; near-fore and off-hind; off-fore. As the off-fore shoulder comes forward you close your hands and legs firmly and with equal pressure. The horse finds it easy to move immediately into the four time walk sequence from the off-fore to: near-hind; near-fore; off-hind; off-fore. The quality of the transition depends entirely on your application of the aids, firmly and accurately at the correct moment. It is a matter of feeling and practice. The transition up helps to develop the carrying capacity of the hocks and this development is furthered by the transitions to canter from the halt and also the rein back. Once again you must realise how easy it is to use the walk only as preparation for the canter transition

THE WALK TO CANTER TRANSITION.

The horse's near hind starts the canter sequence with the off-fore leading. The off-hind and near-fore will move forward together in the second footfall. The third footfall will be with the off-fore as the horse canters to the right. The horse has come slightly above his bit. The rider is seen clearly to be sitting on the inside seat bone.

The near hind started the movement and the picture shows the horse between the second and third footfall. The horse has marked inside flexion in the transition.

The third sequence. The off-fore reaches for the ground to complete the canter sequence.

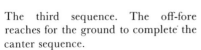

Canter to walk transition. The picture shows clearly that the rider applied her aids just as the leading leg, the off-fore, was in the air. The canter sequence is arrested and the off-fore moves into the second footfall of the walk to be followed by near-hind, near-fore, off-hind, off-fore to complete the walk sequence. The rider's weight has been thrown out of balance in the transition and in turn this has affected the horse's mouth which is open in a slight resistance.

or for any other movement. The horse must be worked at the walk with no turns, pirouettes or canter transitions which tend to excite him and encourage him to anticipate. He has to learn that the walk is a pace in its own right just as much as the trot or the canter and he must be content to remain in that pace calmly and quietly until he has completed his work at the walk.

Practise the transitions from walk to canter until the horse goes from walk to canter calmly and with a clear and definite first canter stride. Guard against the quarters swinging out and concentrate on keeping the horse absolutely straight. In the transition down, you must work out for yourself the necessary degree of closing the hands and legs. Applied too softly, the horse will continue in canter; applied too roughly, the horse will lose his balance and come off the bit. It is far easier to obtain a good transition down if you first ask for a small circle. This immediately brings the horse's hind legs well under him and lightens and elevates the forehand. He is able to make the transition without strain or loss of balance.

COUNTER CANTER

At the canter the horse is dead straight through his body with his head slightly inclined over the leading leg. He is required to maintain this position in counter canter. This means that in counter canter on the right rein the horse leads with the near-fore or outside leg. His head remains slightly bent over the near-fore while his spine follows the straight line to the right. Only his head is inclined over the near-fore, the rest of the horse describes the same straight line throughout his length as shown on a right circle. The hind legs still follow in the tracks of the forelegs.

83

Counter canter in the corner. The horse is leading with the off-fore but is on the left rein and is therefore in counter canter. The rider continues to sit on the right seat bone. The horse's head is slightly inclined over the leading leg but otherwise he follows the line as if he were in true canter.

The horse is not asked at first to canter round the arena in counter canter, with the outside leg leading. This would only confuse him and inevitably throw him off balance in the corners. He has to learn that he must remain on the one leg until he receives further orders, and that he must not offer to change legs simply because of a change of direction which makes him feel he should be leading with the inside foreleg.

The first lesson asks only for a few strides at counter canter and in such a way that the horse scarcely notices that he has done it. You use the school figure of the counter change of hand. A normal counter change of hand is from quarter marker to centre X and back to the next quarter marker, involving three changes of direction. On the left rein first you turn left at the quarter marker, then right at X and then left again at the next quarter marker. At the canter this would involve counter canter from the centre X to the second quarter marker. Do not ask the horse at first for a full counter change of hand by going all the way to X but just for a shallow loop of three to five metres. Be careful to remain sitting on the inside. If you change your weight distribution at the centre of the loop to counteract the counter canter, the horse will become unbalanced and have to struggle to maintain the canter sequence. Your weight remains on the inside and you stress to the horse the aids for cantering with the near-fore or inside leg leading. If the horse breaks into a trot or becomes disunited, straighten him quietly, apply the aids to canter with the inside foreleg leading and try again on the next long side following a shallower loop. Increase the depth of the loop gradually as the horse understands the lesson and becomes more supple. Shortly he will be able to describe a full counter change of hand and then you can progress to three shallow loops of the serpentine to either side of the centre line. Start by making each loop three metres from the line and increase the depth of the loops gradually to five metres.

The next step is to ask the horse for a half circle at counter canter, but give the horse every chance of doing it without difficulty and make it a very large circle. Use the figure eight as the vehicle for your counter canter. Describe a circle to the left as your first part of the figure eight and remain on the near fore as you move on to right circle at X. Do not force the horse to continue on the circle if the canter becomes laboured but move gently from counter canter back to true canter with the near fore leading on the left rein. Practise until the horse can describe more and more of the second circle at counter canter and can ultimately complete a figure of eight on a decreased circle.

Halt to Canter Transitions and Bloquer

The halt to canter transition is relatively simple if the horse is calm and confident already in his transition from walk to canter. Ask him first for a few walk to canter transitions up and down and then halt from the walk. Drive him well into the halt so that he is four-square and his hind legs are well under him. Keep him on the bit and attentive and, after two or three seconds at the halt, apply the aids to canter. Raise the inside hand slightly, vibrating the fingers, and have your weight on the inside. Use your back strongly downwards to press the horse forward from behind. The horse strikes off into the canter without hesitation as long as the halt has not been sustained for too long with the possible loss of forward impulsion.

This work is inclined to make the horse excited, so you must be very cool and very patient and very moderate in your demands. Ask for no more than two or three transitions in a lesson and if the horse strikes off on the wrong leg, return to the walk to canter transition on the correct leg so that the horse becomes more appreciative of the aids for that particular leg. In this case you are using the horse's tendency to anticipate to your own advantage and the horse learns the lesson more easily. After several walk to canter transitions on the one leg the horse will strike off from halt to canter on the same leg without hesitation or difficulty. Let him rest for a few minutes at a free walk on a loose rein and then repeat the exercise on the other rein. Do not attempt to ask for alternate changes until the horse is perfectly sure of the aids and makes no semblance of a mistake in striding into the canter with the required leg leading.

The canter to halt transition is much more difficult and there are few horses in the Three-Day-Event tests who can show a good transition. It cannot be obtained without the use of 'bloquer'. The horse is incapable of halting from the canter unless his hind legs are well under him and he is very light and responsive. He must also be in perfect balance and control and be completely co-ordinated and supple. The bloquer is an extremely effective and strong aid and, applied correctly, will result in the horse stopping absolutely in his tracks. To obtain the bloquer, the back becomes very strong, it is braced into the movement while hands and legs close firmly. You must remember to go with the movement. The transition to halt will be effected immediately if your back, hands and legs are used all at once and you must be ready for the sudden cessation of forward movement. It is very easy to be thrown out of balance if the horse responds instantaneously whereas it is important that you do nothing to interfere with the horse's completion of the movement. Hold the horse in halt for two or three seconds and then give him the aids to canter on with the inside foreleg leading— raise the inside hand slightly, vibrating the fingers, weight on the inside seat bone to push the horse forward from behind. Use the transitions from walk to canter and from canter to walk as preparation for halt to canter and canter to halt. Ask as always in moderation and vary your demands so that the horse does not know what to expect and is therefore unable to anticipate.

SIMPLE CHANGE OF LEG
The simple change is a change of leg at the canter with one or two well defined intervening walk strides before the horse strides off on the other leg. He is already accustomed to the walk to canter transitions and thoroughly understands the aids to canter on either leg. If he is not sure of the aids he will make mistakes by striking off on the wrong leg and soon become totally confused. The easiest way in which to start the lesson is to ride a figure of eight. Taking the left rein, describe a twenty metre circle at one end of the arena with the near-fore leg leading and make the transition to walk two or three steps before reaching X. Allow the horse to proceed in walk calmly and with regular footfalls and then apply the aids to strike off with the off-fore leading on to the right twenty metre circle. Returning to X, repeat the exercise, this time striking off on the near-fore again after a well defined and calm walk. If the horse tends to anticipate, walk the whole of the way

round the circle or even round the figure of eight until he gives up all ideas of cantering. Once he is calm, try again.

Gradually decrease the number of walk strides until the horse is able to perform a simple change of leg with two perfect intervening steps at the walk. By this time he has thoroughly understood the lesson and can repeat it on straight lines and, ultimately, around the arena. This later exercise is not required of a Three-Day-Event horse but demonstrates more fully the horse's appreciation of obedience to the aids while he is in either true or counter canter. He is on the threshold of flying changes and the beginning of High School or *Haute Ecole*.

The horse has now completed all the dressage training required for Three-Day-Eventing but, just like an athlete, he will require to keep his muscles in tone and must continue with the daily practice. From this point, you must follow a programme which bears this in mind. It needs to be only of fifteen or twenty minutes' duration but it must incorporate all the suppling exercises and the work at all the three paces and yet it must avoid the pitfall of boredom.

CHAPTER THIRTEEN

The jumping seat. Preliminary jumping work. Poles on the ground. Cavalletti

The preliminary jumping exercises follow after the section devoted to dressage training. This is for the sake of convenience and easy reference, but the horse can start his jumping programme as soon as he is obedient to the aids. When you are confident that he is calm enough in his work on the ground to be able to undertake the jumping exercises without any excitement or fuss, you can start this programme. In all probability it will coincide with the stage the horse has reached by the end of chapter six or seven.

The two chapters which follow deal with the preliminary work. They advise how to introduce the horse to poles on the ground and cavalletti work and then to a variety of small obstacles. You should follow these exercises even though your horse has been hunted and you know he can jump. It is important that he learns

Perfect bascule and the perfect jumping position. Note the line from elbow through to the horse's mouth and the sympathetic fingers.

Judy Bradwell and Simply Simon.

how to jump correctly and with a developing bascule. Bascule is the perfect arc described by the horse over a fence, rounding his back and using his head and neck freely to follow the line of the half circle from take off to landing.

The jumping seat is entirely different from your dressage seat. There should be a difference of at least two holes in your leathers to shorten the stirrups, your body weight is more forward and your reins are shorter with the arms straighter. At the canter you balance just out of the saddle so that your knee joints are absorbing the movement and are supporting the body in a constant but supple position.

The jumping seat.

The first lesson is simple and straightforward. It deals with poles on the ground and is designed to give the horse confidence and to develop his co-ordination and balance. Remember to work equally on both reins in every lesson.

Start by placing a heavy pole about nine feet long on the ground and walk the horse over this a few times. Do not allow him to jump or rush but insist that he walks calmly over it with no change of pace and then repeat this at the trot. Add another pole, and place it one and a half yards from the first one. Trot quietly up to the two poles in a straight line so that the horse negotiates them in two strides. He must not attempt to jump over the poles and, if this happens, slow down your pace and soothe the horse as he makes his next approach. Keep it all very calm and quiet. When he can trot carefully over the two poles add a third, one and a half yards from the second, so that the spaces are all equidistant. Gradually increase the number of poles until the horse can manage a line of six or eight without hesitation and yet retains calmness and control. You can arrange the poles so that you go along one side of the arena over six and return down the next side over a line of eight. The horse will soon understand the lesson and negotiate each line with a swinging trot and marked rhythm. Obviously, you will have to shorten the width between the poles if your horse is small. One and a half yards is the correct distance for an animal around sixteen hands. It is important in all cases to make sure the poles are equidistant and that you check that they remain so after the horse has rapped them. Sometimes he will make a mistake and step on, rather than over, a pole. At first he will not be perfectly co-ordinated and not know exactly where he is placing his feet. He becomes more accurate as the lesson progresses.

The more time you spend on this early work the more the horse will benefit. He is learning not to rush at the poles and to use his head and neck and his back properly. The muscles over his loins begin to develop with the new exercise and he gains strength in that all important area behind the saddle. Once he has mastered the lines of poles he can progress to cavaletti work. Again, the accent is on developing muscle power and achieving a calm and quiet approach by gradual and systematic exercises.

Cavalletti are of Italian origin and a cavalletto is a strong pole bolted at each end on to a crossbar. The crossbar is angled so that it affords three different heights for the bolted pole, the crosses at either end providing the support. The intervening pole is approximately nine feet long. The lowest height of the cavelletto is set when the pole is under the cross; the middle height when the cavalletto is rolled over so that the pole is on the nearside or offside of the cross; and it is at its highest when the pole is rolled over again and is on top of the cross.

Cavalletti work makes the horse even more supple and develops his co-ordination and balance a stage further. The aim is for the horse to be able to trot down a line of six or eight cavalletti at their lowest height. This will mean he has to use himself considerably, elevating his trot and flexing his joints to a marked degree. The back swings from side to side with the diagonal movement. Approach the poles or cavelletti always in a dead straight line and aim for the centre. Use the sitting trot and remain sitting until well after the last pole before beginning to rise. If you are working in an arena, use rising trot round the arena and sitting trot at the start of the long side where the poles are placed. Begin to rise again on the short side of the arena. Allow the horse to have full use of his head and neck while trotting over the poles or cavalletti and sit into and with the movement with your weight perfectly distributed. Your stirrups should be two holes higher in this work than they are for the dressage training.

It will be a great deal easier if you have an assistant standing by during the preliminary and, indeed, all the jumping work. Apart from the time factor, it is also very frustrating to have to dismount and mount continually to attend to the poles or fences. Further-more, it becomes too great a temptation not to take the trouble to check that the distances between the poles remain equal at all times and to curtail a lesson when the horse would benefit from more work. If you have someone there to look after the poles and cavalletti, and later the fences, you are much more likely to be thorough and patient. The difference between success and failure often depends on whether or not you take the trouble to do the job properly. This approach applies to the whole of the work in this book and I shall return to it in a later chapter to stress its importance.

The first introduction to a cavalletto comes at the end of a line of poles. Ride the horse over six poles on the ground once or twice to ensure he is relaxed and calm, yet is using himself properly and with accuracy. Do not attempt to 'place' him at the first pole except to make sure you are aiming for a straight line down the middle. Allow him to work out for himself how to arrive at the correct distance from the beginning of the line by adjusting his stride so that he can negotiate it easily and with equal strides. Having ridden successfully over the six, replace the last pole with a cavalletto and approach again. The horse may attempt a little jump over the sixth pole, now raised off the ground as a cavalletto. If he does this, quietly restrain him and continue round the arena in slow trot. Trot over another set of poles on the ground on the other side of the arena and, even when the other line is gradually replaced by six cavalletti, let these remain on the ground. They give the horse a reminder of the first lesson and act as a calming and reassuring influence whilst he absorbs the new exercise. When he negotiates the last pole—now a cavalletto—easily, replace the penultimate pole on the ground with a cavalletto, and continue to do this until you have a line of six cavalletti, and then add a seventh and lastly an eighth.

You must be patient and only replace the poles gradually. If you are in too great a hurry or too enthusiastic, you may ask the horse for too much, too soon. He has only to make one bad mistake in the middle of the cavalletti to frighten himself thoroughly and to put you back considerably as far as confidence and calmness are concerned. As always, you must be content to progress slowly and carefully. You want the horse to have absolute confidence in you; this has to be earned and will grow as the horse realises he is never asked to do anything of which he is not capable. Obedience to your wishes must never result in his landing in trouble and so it is your responsibility to realise the dangers and to think carefully about any obstacles he has to face.

CHAPTER FOURTEEN

Developing the horse's athletic ability. Small fences and combinations

The horse is now ready to face small obstacles but you should start by incorporating them with poles on the ground and cavalletti. You retain the poles and cavalletti to remind the horse that there is no reason for excitement or anxiety. Your aim is to get him jumping quietly without thinking of it as an exciting innovation or as an excuse to misbehave, but merely as a natural extension of the first lesson.

Keep a line of poles on the ground down one side of the arena and on the other side place three poles set one and a half yards (1·35 metres) apart in front of a two feet high (60 cm.) post and rails. The rails are twenty-one feet (6·40 metres) away from the third pole on the ground. The idea is for the horse to trot over the poles on the ground, take one non-jumping stride and pop out over the rail. He resumes the trot as soon as possible after landing. This method of approach means that the horse, as ever, has to remain quiet and careful over the poles. He arrives at the correct place for take-off by virtue of the twenty-one feet (6·40 metres) interval and is perfectly placed to bascule beautifully over the obstacle. The whole thing is calm and collected and must remain so over the single obstacles.

Next you teach the horse to jump small fences out of a trot with no poles leading up to them. Erect three fences in the arena, one along the centre line and one on each diagonal each about two feet (60 cm) in height. The fence on the centre line re-affirms the lesson you have just taught the horse and has the three poles in front of it with an intervening space of twenty-four feet (7m. 30) between the last pole and the fence. On each diagonal place a small post and rails that can be jumped from either direction. Use heavy poles from the beginning so that the horse learns to respect his fences and acquires the habit of jumping cleanly. All horses jump better over imposing obstacles and will make a bigger effort. They dislike 'empty' fences with a lot of daylight showing.

In the early lessons you are restricted with the type of obstacles you build because they must be small in height, but you can make sure the poles are solid and not easy to dislodge. In this way the horse will assume that all fences are equally hard to knock down and that it is not a good idea to hit them. This early appreciation may well influence his whole jumping life. As the lessons progress you can begin to introduce tiny walls and gates and rustic as well as coloured bars in the forms of both upright and spread fences. The new fences should not worry the horse because they are so small and he does not have to make a great effort to jump them. In this manner he becomes increasingly confident and accustoms himself immediately to a fresh obstacle. Confidence comes first and is your prime consideration; developing the height and spread of the obstacles is only a matter of time and will follow imperceptibly.

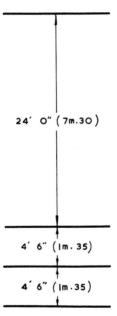

24′ 0″ (7m.30)

4′ 6″ (1m. 35)

4′ 6″ (1m.35)

Layout of the combination of three poles in front of the small fence, and the two small fences placed on the diagonals.

The two fences on the diagonals should consist initially of simple post and rails about two feet (60 cm.) high. Place them carefully (see fig above) so that they can be jumped in either direction yet do not interfere with the approach to the poles and fence along the centre line.

The lesson proceeds at the trot and you start by circling at the bottom of the arena before turning down the centre line towards the poles on the ground and the post and rails. The horse will break into a canter stride as he negotiates the third pole and approaches the post and rails. The twenty-four feet (7m. 30) interval gives him room for one perfect non-jumping stride before he bascules correctly over the two feet (60 cm.) rail. Settle him back into a trot, circle calmly at the top end of the arena and then approach one of the fences placed on the diagonal, from right to left if you are on a right circle, and from left to right if you are on a left circle.

Remember that calmness is your aim and if the horse shows any signs of rushing, turn off from the fence. Turning off means that immediately you feel the horse losing the rhythm of approach and wanting to rush towards the jump, you turn the horse left or right on to a ten or fifteen metres circle. Circle until the horse regains his rhythm and calmness and then approach the fence for your next attempt. At the slightest sign of rushing, turn off again and repeat it every time until the horse approaches quietly and calmly. Reward him as soon as he pops over the obstacle and settles back into his ordinary trot. As always in your training, remember to circle on both reins in turning off, first one way and then the other. The horse must never be allowed to anticipate your demands but must learn to wait for your instructions and then carry them out obediently and calmly.

Once the horse has jumped the fence on the centre line, and then the one on the diagonal, you can negotiate the three fences as a little course. Circle left at the bottom, turn down the centre line, circle right at the top once and then jump the fence on the diagonal. Allow the horse to lapse into the canter only on the take off stride and resume the trot as soon as possible after he lands. Circle left at the bottom of the arena, turn down the centre again and circle left at the top. Then jump the fence on the other diagonal.

After this you can jump the two fences on the diagonals from either side. Do not attempt to come down the centre line in reverse as it would only confuse the horse and nothing would be gained from the exercise. Remember throughout the lesson to reward the horse whenever he jumps well and cleanly, and to say 'NO' if he rushes or if he rattles or knocks down a fence. Do not allow him to get bored by too much jumping. It must always be a joy to him and remain interesting to the end of the lesson. On the other hand, you must not give him so much to think about that he is unable to cope with it all and your enthusiasm results, not in his education progressing a stage further, but in his developing an evasion or resistance. It is a matter of deciding just how much the horse can take at one time and you will only learn this crucial balance by application and experience. Meanwhile, use your commonsense and, above all, be patient.

The three fences in the arena can develop slowly in size and scope so that the horse can jump small spreads and uprights

Jumping must always be a joy to the horse.
Sheila Willcox with Fair and Square.

without difficulty. Add another post and rails to one of the fences to make it a spread fence, but keep the first rail lower than the second for a few lessons so that the horse can see the spread easily and learns to negotiate it. Later on it can become a true parallel. The other fence on the diagonal can remain an upright but you can introduce the horse to crossbars, to a small gate or wall or a little brush fence with a rail above it.

The fence along the centre line provides the horse with his first introduction to combinations. A comfortable distance for the horse to take one non-jumping stride at a slow speed is twenty-four feet (7·30 metres), so you place a second post and rails twenty-four feet away behind the first rail. The horse then trots over the three poles on the ground, takes one non-jumping stride and bascules over the first rail; he lands, takes one non-jumping stride, and takes off over the second rail. Make sure you keep the horse dead straight down the poles on the ground and over the first rail and then you should have no difficulty in completing the combination. Reward him as soon as he jumps it well and remember to turn off just before the obstacle if he begins to rush on the approach.

The combination fence develops so that it is either two upright fences, one upright followed by a spread, a spread followed by an

95

upright, or two spread fences. While the horse is absorbing these new combinations the intervening distance remains at twenty-four feet (7·30 metres), and for two non-jumping strides it is thirty-four feet (10·35 metres). Obviously this is influenced by the slow speed at which the horse is going and the subject is dealt with in greater detail in the chapter on show jumping and cross-country. At this stage you are concerned only with introducing the horse to combinations so that he remains confident and willing. Do not attempt the more difficult distances until the horse can jump a low two- or three-fence combination with either one or two easy non-jumping strides in between.

CHAPTER FIFTEEN

Developing the horse's ability and confidence. The speeds for show jumping, the steeplechase and cross-country. 'True' distances. How to assess your stride. The 'bounce' stride

The horse must now learn to adapt himself to more difficult distances between obstacles and to adjust his stride accordingly. You teach him to do this very gradually and only over small fences at first. The early jumping lessons from the introductory poles on the ground to the start of the show jumping courses require a great deal of time and attention and the horse will benefit enormously if you allow him to consolidate this training over a period of two or three months. During this time he gains tremendous confidence in his own ability and faith in his rider. This faith in you must be

The horse must have absolute confidence in his rider and be ready to tackle any obstacle.

Sheila Willcox with Here and Now.

carefully nurtured and established so that throughout his jumping career the horse has absolute confidence in your judgement and will tackle any obstacle no matter how terrifying it may appear to him. You must realise the importance of this point and never ask the horse to jump any fence which is beyond his capabilities or to do anything at all which results in him hurting or frightening himself. He should believe in you implicitly as his rider and be prepared to go anywhere and do anything that you ask.

In the early jumping lessons he develops his jumping muscles which may never have been used until now, and he becomes considerably more agile and athletic. The fact that the fences remain less than 3 ft. 3 in. (1 metre) means that he is never over-faced, yet he learns to use himself correctly and to the best of his ability by reason of the siting of the obstacles and by jumping them out of a trot. He can start to canter over the obstacles once he has completed the work in chapter 14, but you must continue to insist on calmness and the correct approach and never allow him to rush or become excited.

Follow the same rule of turning off from a fence if he begins to rush at it, and if ever he runs out at a fence, stop him as quickly as you can. If he has run out to the left, turn him strongly to the right, and if he runs out to the right, turn him back to the left before your next attempt. Although the horse needs his head and neck free during the bascule, you must not drop his head on the approach. Maintain contact all the time and keep him well between hands and legs. Go with the movement over a fence and try to keep your lower arms in a straight line from elbow through to the horse's mouth. Allow your fingers to open over the fence to give maximum freedom while retaining the lightest contact.

The horse progresses slowly from jumping the initial three fences to a little course incorporating a variety of obstacles, none of them measuring more than 3 ft. 3 in. (1 metre). Add to the obstacles until you have about seven of them, including a double and a treble. Slowly increase the heights and the spreads. You can begin over the small introductory course at a trot and allow the horse to break into a canter whenever he likes. Go back to the trot if he threatens to become excited, but if the preparatory work has been thorough he will remain perfectly calm and attentive. Once he is settled and confident in this preliminary work, he can begin to jump the small fences at gradually increasing angles. Begin with a very slight angle of approach and never waver nor allow the horse to think he can run past the fence. Make it perfectly clear to him that he is to jump the obstacle and keep a strong contact up to the moment of take off.

Next, he must learn to adjust his stride and to do this you vary the intervening distances between the combination fences. First you should realise the different speeds demanded in the different phases and how they will affect the horse's manner of jumping. A horse's average stride, between obstacles at the normal show jumping speeds of 327 yards per minute (300 metres) or 382 yards per minute (350 metres), is 11 ft. 6 in. (3·50 metres). The correct take off position for a fence is one and a third times the height away from the obstacle, and the horse can still jump the fence safely by taking off either side of this ideal position within a zone measuring one quarter of the height of the fence. Therefore, if the fence measures 4 ft. (1m. 22) in height, the ideal take off would be 5 ft. 3 in. (1m. 60) away from the fence. The margin of safety would be 6 in. (15 cm.) either side of the take off position. It means that to jump a fence of 4 ft. (1m. 22) the horse can take off safely between 5 ft. 9 in. (1m. 75) and 4 ft. 9 in. (1m. 45) in front of the obstacle (1m. 75).

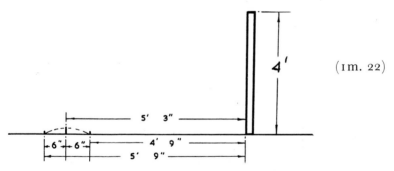

The correct take off position for a 4 ft fence is one and a third times the height away from the obstacle.

There is a considerable difference in the required speeds for the show jumping phase between the novice class horses and those in the advanced class. The open-intermediate, intermediate and novice class tests are carried out at 327 yards per minute (300 metres). In a Three-Day-Event the speed is from 382 yards per minute (350 metres) to 436 yards per minute (400 metres), and at an International meeting the speed is 436 yards per minute (400 metres).

At this point you should also appreciate the difference between the show jumping speeds and those for the steeplechase and cross-country phases of a Three-Day-Event. In order to obtain no penalties in the steeplechase phase, you have to complete the course at a speed of 755 yards per minute (690 metres), and to remain unpenalised in the cross-country phase you must complete the course at a speed of 624 yards per minute (570 metres). There is obviously a considerable difference between the show jumping speeds and those for the steeplechase and cross-country, and you will appreciate the extent to which your horse must adapt himself to a completely different way of jumping. Over the steeplechase and the more straightforward of the cross-country fences he must stand off and jump out of his stride. In the show jumping phase he has to jump with accuracy and precision. He takes off much nearer to his fences, showing a perfect bascule with an arched back.

The show jumping fences will not exceed 4 ft. (1·22 metres) in height, 11 ft. 6 in. (3 metres) over a spread, and will not exceed a spread of 6 ft. (1·80 metres) at the highest point and 9 ft 3 in. (2·80 metres) at the base in obstacles with both height and spread.

TRUE DISTANCES
There are certain 'true' distances, and once you know these distances you can move the combination fences so that the horse has to shorten or to lengthen his stride.

The 'true' distances over two verticals are as follows:
One non-jumping stride—26 ft. (8 metres)
Two non-jumping strides—36 ft. (11 metres)
Three non-jumping strides—49 ft. (15 metres)
Four non-jumping strides—59 ft. (18 metres)
Five non-jumping strides—71 ft. (21·60 metres)
Six non-jumping strides—82 ft. (25 metres)

In principle, you create a short distance by reducing the 'true' distance by 1 ft. (30 cm.) or 1 ft. 6 in. (45 cm.). You create a long distance by increasing the 'true' distance by 1 ft. (30 cm.) or 2 ft. (60 cm.). The fewer the intervening strides between fences, the smaller the variation from the 'true' distance.

You can set the fences either with two short distances or two long ones, or by a 'true' distance followed by a long one—where the horse must be ridden strongly after landing over the first obstacle.

Distances are affected by:
(i) Going downhill. Here the stride lengthens, and the 'true' distance should be increased.
(ii) Going uphill. Here the stride shortens, and the 'true' distance should be decreased.
(iii) Heavy going. The horse's stride shortens.
(iv) Ideal going. The horse's stride lengthens.
(v) A restricted area. The horse's stride shortens. Conversely, it lengthens in an open area.

Below, you will find a set of diagrams to illustrate the various distances over combination fences with one and two non-jumping strides:

   (i) two verticals
  (ii) one vertical and one true parallel or one square oxer
 (iii) one true parallel or one square oxer and one vertical
 (iv) two true parallels or two square oxers
  (v) one vertical and one ascending oxer
 (vi) one ascending oxer and one vertical
 (vii) two ascending oxers
(viii) one ascending oxer and one true parallel or one square oxer

'True' distances. The diagrams show two distances between the various combinations. The first is for one non-jumping stride, the second for two non-jumping strides.

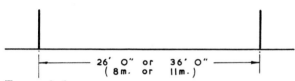

Two verticals.

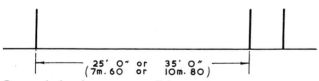

One vertical and one true parallel or square oxer.

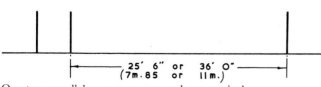

One true parallel or square oxer and one vertical.

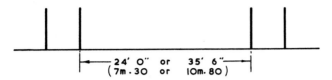

24' 0" or 35' 6"
(7m.30 or 10m.80)

Two true parallels or two square oxers.

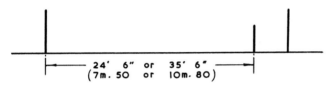

24' 6" or 35' 6"
(7m.50 or 10m.80)

One vertical and one ascending oxer.

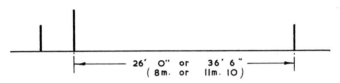

26' 0" or 36' 6"
(8m. or 11m.10)

One ascending oxer and one vertical.

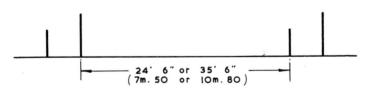

24' 6" or 35' 6"
(7m.50 or 10m.80)

Two ascending oxers.

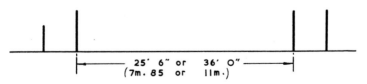

25' 6" or 36' 0"
(7m.85 or 11m.)

One ascending oxer and one true parallel or square oxer.

Always measure the distance from inside to inside—from the landing side of the one fence to the take off side of the next. Treat the hog's back type of obstacle or a round chicken coop as a vertical fence and measure to its highest point.

It is the one-, two- and three-stride combination fences which require the most attention and practice. The longer the intervening distance, the more time you have to regulate the stride. In the shorter distances, requiring up to three strides only, it is important that you should know how to ride your horse so that you can negotiate any double or treble combination safely. You must discover if your horse's stride matches the requirements for jumping the 'true' distances. Set up a fence of two verticals 26 ft. (8 metres) apart and check that he jumps it with one easy, non-jumping stride. Set it at 36 ft. (11 metres) apart and check that he has two easy non-jumping strides. If his stride in the middle is too long he will be too close to the next fence and you must ride into that particular distance on a shorter stride. Conversely, if he lands short and in one stride is too far away to attempt to take off for the second fence, you must approach the distance of this combination on a longer stride. Each horse needs individual attention and it is up to you to discover how he varies from the 'true' distances and to know how to ride him so that he can cope with them without trouble.

THE 'BOUNCE' STRIDE

He must learn also to jump a 'bounce' fence. This is a combination of two fences where the horse lands over the first fence and takes off immediately—with no intervening stride—over the next. Provided that he has worked systematically up to this point, he will be supple enough and confident enough to manage it at his first attempt. The distance between the two fences starts at 12 ft. (3m. 66) and the maximum distance to be attempted as a 'bounce' fence is 18 ft. (5m. 48). This 18 ft. 'bounce' is only for a very experienced and bold horse who is tremendously confident. He has to be ridden at the fence with speed, in the knowledge that he will 'bounce' and will not try to put in a non-jumping stride.

During the training described in this chapter you must also begin to work over natural obstacles as an introduction to cross-country fences. Start by jumping the horse over small hedges and popping across well-defined ditches. Continue to keep the horse calm and sensible in his approach and jump at the pace you dictate rather than at the speed the horse prefers. Gradually increase the size of the hedges and ditches and move on to larger spreads and to an open ditch in front of a hedge and a hedge with a ditch behind it. Introduce the horse to a coffin-type obstacle—a post and rails, then one non-jumping stride before a ditch, and another non-jumping stride before a second post and rails. Always keep the fence low when the horse is facing it as a new obstacle. Allow him to realise how it is to be negotiated when it is small and while consequently it requires little jumping effort.

In this way the horse's confidence increases until eventually he believes he can tackle anything you ask him to jump. It is tremendously important that you always work with this point in mind. Your enjoyment in the present is of little consideration. Rather than gallop towards an unknown but inviting-looking fence just out of sheer high spirits, you must jump only the obstacles you have inspected and know are perfectly safe. You must jump nothing in practice which may trap the horse through no fault of his own. Establishing and preserving his absolute confidence in your judgement is of paramount importance and your practice work must always be done with this in mind.

CHAPTER SIXTEEN

The event season. A graduated programme to introduce the horse first to one-day-events and then to three-day-events

The process of getting a horse fit for the actual events is as gradual and systematic as the dressage or jumping training and is of equal importance. The horse must be produced for an event at the necessary stage of physical and mental fitness and this is achieved only by adhering strictly to a carefully designed training programme. Horses are surprisingly delicate creatures for their size and weight and it is no easy task to avoid some form of leg trouble during the long preparation. The Three-Day-Event horse has to be as fit as a Grand National runner. More than this, he must be so well-trained and mentally well-balanced that he can produce a calm and accurate dressage test at a time when he is at peak fitness. He must be taught to behave himself during his dressage lessons regardless of how ebullient he feels. Luckily, he is a creature of habit and you use this to your advantage.

The daily dressage lessons should take place always when he first comes out of his box. Start your dressage straight away instead of taking the easy way out and riding him on the roads for half an hour to get his back down. The horse must learn from the start that he does his dressage first and for the duration of that lesson he must be thoroughly obedient and attentive. Never allow him to buck or kick or misbehave in any way during this period even though you realise it is only high spirits. You must be absolutely firm and consistent about this, stopping any exhibition as soon as it starts. In this way, the horse realises he is always required to behave himself for the first half hour of the exercise.

At the end of his dressage lesson he can be rewarded with a little fun. He will appreciate this and soon get to know the programme. Differentiate still further between the absolute obedience and attention you demand during the dressage lesson and the subsequent relaxed period. Always finish the dressage with a good halt on the centre line and go out of the arena on a loose rein just as if you were finishing a test. Make much of your horse, dismount and give him a handful of grass or some other reward. Shorten your leathers a couple of holes to the length used for long exercise and jumping and then remount. Now the horse can enjoy himself for a few minutes and you can canter round the field or over a little fence. Anything to relax him thoroughly and to encourage him to enjoy life and to like his work. Obviously this is all done within reason and you do not go off at a mad gallop nor do you incite the horse to fling himself all over the field. He will feel your different seat immediately and notice your change of attitude. He learns how far he can go so that both of you appreciate and enjoy the few minutes of exuberance.

The actual training programme to make sure the horse is fit enough to take part in a One-Day-Event covers twelve weeks and the work consists of daily dressage and road work, some jumping practice and, lastly, fast work during the last few weeks. It starts with a total of one hour's work a day during the first week and builds up to two and a half hour's work by the twelfth week. The ideal routine for an event horse is based on the realisation that Trials are extraordinarily demanding and that you must conserve your horse if he is to last more than a season or two. There is a great wastage of event horses through the inevitable leg trouble and in the majority of cases it happens either because they competed when they were not fit enough or because their owners were too ambitious or greedy and the horses took part in too many Trials without a proper rest.

The absolutely ideal plan in producing a young horse for Trials would be to spend at least six, and preferably nine, months on the basic dressage work and the preliminary jumping. At the end of this time, and assuming he has all the attributes in his favour, the horse is well into the second stage of training. He is developing the carrying capacity of the hocks and is established in his work as described in chapters one to eight. He is well grounded in his jumping and is capable of negotiating a small course of varied obstacles with a good bascule and in a proper attitude. Having reached this stage he should have a complete rest before starting on an actual Trials season. He should be roughed off and turned out in the field for anything from three to six weeks.

Bearing in mind that the season is split into two parts, starting in March and again in August, the horse must be ready to begin his training in early January or in May, twelve weeks before the first event. He will need three weeks of walking exercise on the roads before this to harden his legs and to allow his constitution to become accustomed to the change from field to stable. As soon as he comes in he should be wormed with one of the modern preparations. Multiwurma deals with all kinds of worms and bots and is tasteless. The worm dose should be repeated every six months once the horse has been thoroughly cleaned out.

The horse starts his first year in Trials with novice events and if he has been well schooled and is properly fit he is likely to move up into the Intermediate grade by the end of the season. This is a point that needs considerable attention. You do not want the horse upgraded out of novice events before he is ready to face the larger and more demanding obstacles of the intermediate class, so you must know exactly how close your horse is to becoming inter- mediate and make sure you do not allow him to gain the re- maining points too soon. Most of the competitors have to rely on the actual events to gain their cross-country experience and, unless you are lucky enough to have every sort of obstacle at your dis- posal at home, you must be extremely cautious. The horse needs at least three or four runs in novice classes before he is ready to face the bigger fences, and he will benefit enormously from being given an 'easy' run on his first time out. This applies to a well- trained horse and an experienced rider, and the less experienced combinations should remain as novices for a minimum six events.

Apart from his participation in Trials, the horse should continue his general education and you should enter in jumper classes and local shows to provide him with the all-important show jumping practice. He will also gain valuable experience in working hunter classes and even in show classes. All these things further his education and help him to accept travelling and strange sur- roundings as a matter of course.

The autumn season begins in August and, assuming that the horse is to start eventing then, he will begin his twelve-week training programme in May. Choose your events carefully and take particular notice of the posting dates for entries. Take the trouble to fill in the forms well in advance and to keep them safely so that they are ready to send by the first post on the opening day. Take particular notice of which dressage test applies to which event and learn them thoroughly. Your horse should be capable of taking part in one event a week on average and could do three events within ten days, provided there was no great travelling distance involved. A horse is usually able to produce good form the day after he has made a big effort. He is at a much lower ebb forty- eight hours after an event and should not be asked to do much on this day.

The autumn season finishes in October and as soon as possible after this the horse should be given a rest. Hunting is a superb medium for gaining cross-country experience but the event horse cannot do both jobs at once. He needs a complete break during

November and December and begins to get fit again soon after Christmas. Ideally, the horse should have gained his hunting experience before he embarks on his Trials' career, for the two simply do not mix.

In the spring the horse should complete in as many events as possible. The aim is for him to take part in his first Three-Day-Event in May for this event is far less severe than either Badminton or Burghley and is the perfect introduction. The horse will then be ready to compete at Burghley in the autumn and at Badminton the following year if he shows himself capable of dealing with the additional demands of his first Three-Day-Event, and proves his speed and endurance. The combination of the introductory Three-Day-Event in May and Burghley in September means that in his first full year there is not enough time to give the horse a complete summer rest. Nevertheless it is of vital importance that he has a short break and, at the end of May, as soon as he returns from his first Three-Day-Event, he should go out into the field for a few hours every day. This can continue for two weeks and has the advantage of allowing the horse the necessary rest while making sure he does not become too soft. He will be ready to resume training in June, in preparation for Burghley in September.

The second full year sets the pattern which should be followed with an open event horse. The main aims are the Three-Day-Events at Badminton and Burghley and, to give the horse the very best chance of success, he should have two rest periods during the twelve months. The first is for four weeks immediately after the spring Three-Day-Event and the second after the last autumn event in October when he has six to eight weeks rest. This ensures that the horse retains his interest in the sport and goes a long way towards keeping him sound. Only a mentally well-balanced horse of sound constitution is likely to remain in top eventing for more than two years and it pays not to be too greedy. No horse can remain at peak fitness from March until October. He grows tired and stale working all this time and when that happens he makes mistakes. You must guard against this.

CHAPTER SEVENTEEN

The training programme itself. Daily dressage and road work. Jumping practice. Fast work. The necessary speeds for no time penalties. The training chart. The feed chart

At the end of this chapter you will find the training programme and a feed chart. Set up the Training Programme in the tack room and the Feed Chart in the fodder room. Tick off each days work as it is completed. If anything happens to prevent the horse from working, enter it on the chart, and in this way you will have a complete record of the work your horse has done and know exactly how much he has missed. You can alter the rest day to suit your own particular requirements, but it is important to work the horse at approximately the same time each day. He will thrive much better if he is secure in a routine and you will note that the feed chart is graduated in the same way as the training programme. Feeding the horse today has been made a great deal easier by the availability of balanced compound feeds in cube form. They were introduced by Spillers in 1958 and can be used either by themselves or in association with the more traditional oats and bran mixture. One of the great advantages of cube feeding is that the product is consistent in quality and nutrient value. A horse often accepts more readily a combination of alternate cube feeds and oats feeds. In this way he is more likely to retain his interest in his food and to assimilate the high level of protein intake necessary for the training programme.

Four feeds a day are the most suitable plan for the horse. He does far better if he is fed little and often and it is well worth the extra trouble involved in giving him the late feed at ten o'clock. You should automatically check the horse at the same time and see that there is nothing amiss before he is left for the night.

The chart applies to a horse of 16 h.h. to 16·3 h.h. and you must adjust it slightly to apply to a smaller or a larger animal. The main consideration is not to overface the horse with too much food but to give him just enough to keep him on his feed and to make sure it will enable him to do everything that is required of him. He should be watched carefully to see that his condition is commensurate with the stage of training he has reached. He should look big and well when first he comes in to start his programme. The graduated and systematic long exercise will reduce and remove the excess weight and convert some of it into valuable muscle. The horse must develop strong and hard muscles on his neck, his shoulders, his loins and his quarters and he will be more likely to do this if he starts with a bit of weight on him.

By the end of the first four weeks he should begin to look harder altogether and his skin should be supple and smooth. You should be able to pick it up easily between your fingers. By the time he starts to gallop, in the ninth week, he should look much more taut and show no signs of carrying excess weight. The galloping programme will complete the transformation from a healthy looking animal in near show condition to a hard, fit horse ready to run in a good race.

Use the best hard hay you can find and keep the horse on the same hay throughout his training programme. In ordinary work, the horse has three feeds a day, and 10 or 12 lb of hay split into one third in the morning and two thirds at tea time. Once the training programme starts he needs less hay and, during weeks one to eight his ration is 10 lb. a day split into one third and two thirds as before. The ration is further reduced to 8 lb. a day from week nine to week twelve and is fed exactly as in the previous weeks. Do not allow the horse to eat his straw and sprinkle his bed with disinfectant if he threatens to do this. Alternatively, fit him with a muzzle. It is very important to keep his stomach tight and he must not be allowed to fill himself with bulk.

On the day before his rest day he should have a bran mash made up of 3 lb. of broad bran with a tablespoon of iodised salt, 2 tablespoons of black treacle, and 2 pints of boiling water. Pour the boiling water over the mixture, stir well and then cover with a thick towel for twenty minutes before feeding. Give the bran mash at the 10 p.m. feed. On the rest day itself, feed the horse only three times. This gives his digestion a rest and makes him more keen to eat next day when he returns to his proper work.

Give him a boiled feed twice a week made up of whole oats and whole linseed, or whole oats, linseed and barley. The night before he has a boiled feed, place $1\frac{1}{2}$ lb. of whole oats and a cupful of whole linseed in a saucepan or container and fill it with water. Allow it to soak overnight and cook it very slowly with a lid on all the next day. Give the horse half a cup of barley for the second boiled feed of the week and reduce the linseed this time to half a cup. Cook it with the whole oats in exactly the same way. Feed this to the horse when it is still warm either at 6 p.m. or 10 p.m. and mix it with $1\frac{1}{2}$ to 2 lb. of broad bran.

The work the horse does and the food he eats are completely interdependent. The daily ration of oats increases as the work becomes harder and of longer duration. Conversely, the less the horse does, the smaller the ration of oats he needs and the moment the horse has to be taken off work you must cut down his high protein intake.

Throughout the training programme the horse starts his work with half an hour's dressage lesson. Until he is a proven open eventer he will be continuing his dressage education whilst he is on the getting fit programme. This will keep him interested as he is learning something new the whole time. The open eventer is a different matter, for his education has been completed and he has nothing new to learn. Under these circumstances the rider has to exert all his tact and ingenuity. He must retain the horse's interest. Without this, the vital spark so necessary to earn good marks in a dressage test is lost. This is where the rider's ability to 'feel' is tested for he must be able to appreciate when the horse needs a break. He should notice the very moment when the dressage work shows the first signs of staleness and decide immediately whether or not the horse will benefit from a few days away from the arena.

This departure from the training programme applies only to the proven horse who knows all the work required in the Three-Day-Event test and his daily dressage is therefore just the means of keeping him in practice. The horse is almost certain to become stale at some time during the twelve-week period. The rider must appreciate when that moment is approaching and also to differentiate between the time the horse is being naughty or uncooperative and when he is genuinely bored with his work and needs a change.

After a few days holiday from his dressage, he will return to it with renewed zest and vigour. In an effort to prevent excessive boredom, the rider must work through the daily routine systematically but without undue repetition. The horse must work well and to the very best of his ability but there is no need to continue for the full half hour once the routine has been completed. On some days he will complete the work in ten or fifteen minutes and this is long enough provided the horse has gone well. The remaining fifteen or twenty minutes of the allotted time is simply added on to the road work.

The novice and intermediate grade horses have no such problem and the only pitfall to avoid with them is that of continuing to teach the horse new exercises right up to the day of competition. You do not want the horse to have too much to think about, and to expect him to absorb new lessons and to find himself in strange surroundings all within the space of a few days is to invite trouble. Everything you do throughout the training is executed with the aim of keeping the horse calm and confident. Allow him to work only on well-established work for the week previous to an event. Guard against the horse anticipating the test. It is surprising how very quickly he will learn a sequence of movements and to ride the complete test at home more than once is a bad mistake. You can make sure you know the test thoroughly by riding the whole thing at a trot or even at a walk so that you get the pattern firmly in your mind. Practise various parts of the test out of context but never allow the horse to know what is coming next. Practise also the entry up the centre line and a good halt at varying places on it. Hold the halt each time for several seconds so that the horse is not anticipating the move off almost as soon as he halts. Practise your salute and do not hurry it.

Each day start to work on a different rein from the previous day. Make it a rule to take the left rein on Mondays, Wednesdays and Fridays, and the right rein on the alternate days. In this way your horse has no chance of anticipating the turn at the top of the arena and each day you are starting to work through your dressage routine on a different rein. Work out a definite routine for the dressage period and include all the exercises the horse has learned, first on one rein and then on the other. Precede the lesson always with several minutes of ordinary trot round the arena on both reins. This wears off the horse's freshness and you begin to get the hind legs underneath the horse in preparation for his lesson.

The road work, or long exercise, is the main medium for bringing the horse to peak fitness. In the first two weeks, and especially if the horse has been out at grass for a rest, you should keep to level ground. Slow work up long hills is superb for later on in the programme, but in the early stages you want the horse to work with as little strain as possible. This point should remain in your mind throughout the training. Never subject the horse to any demand which is not commensurate with the stage of his training. You may be tempted to jump him before his legs are hard enough or to compete before he is fit enough to do so without risk. Try to be objective in your approach and do nothing which involves the horse in too great an effort out of context. Only by drawing up a careful training programme and adhering rigidly to this will you be doing all you can to avoid the dangers of leg trouble and standing a good chance of producing your horse perfectly sound and one hundred per cent fit for the events.

The long exercise periods provide opportunities of furthering the horse's general education, and he becomes used to traffic when he goes out on the roads and to opening and shutting gates and coping with undulating ground and different going when the work is over tracks and farmland. The first three weeks are restricted to work at the walk and the trot, and your trotting periods—especially on the hard roads—should be of only a few minutes' duration. After the third week you can introduce a short canter but choose your ground carefully and keep the horse balanced and short. The trotting times are gradually increased as the weeks progress and by the eleventh and twelfth weeks the horse is trotting for ten minutes at a time. Work up to this very slowly, and in the same way build up the canter to a maximum five minutes a time.

The next thing to require attention is the problem of weight. Except in novice events all riders must carry a minimum weight of 165 lbs for the show jumping and cross-country phases. The ideal is for you to be as close as possible to this weight with your saddle. If you are too heavy then try to lose a few pounds but do not over-do it and make yourself too weak to help the horse. If you weigh less than 165 lbs with your saddle, you must make up the weight with lead. The horse has to become accustomed to this extra weight, particularly when he is jumping, and you must remember to carry the weight cloth whenever you practise over fences and also on the occasions when you are making a time check in preparation for a Three-Day-Event. You will need at least one practice for the steeplechase phase in order to work out the necessary speed, and it usually is possible to obtain permission from the relevant authorities to ride over your local point-to-point fences or steeplechase course after a meeting.

The speed for no penalty points over the steeplechase phase is 755 yards a minute (690 metres). This is the equivalent of twenty-six miles an hour (690 metres a minute). Time yourself over a set distance or follow a vehicle travelling at twenty-six miles an hour until you have the feel of the speed and can reproduce it to order.

The minimum cross-country speed is 624 yards per minute (570 metres). It is a fast canter at twenty-one and a half miles an hour (570 metres a minute) and to finish a course with no time penalties you have to keep up a consistently good speed. Checking into a fence loses valuable seconds and you cannot afford to waste time in turning or to take any of the easier alternative fences if you intend to finish without time penalties.

The speed for the Roads and Tracks is 262 yards per minute (240 metres) or nine miles an hour (240 metres per minute). This is the pace of a good, free trot. Even this speed should be checked. You must be sure that the horse is capable of keeping up the speed over the distances of phases A and C in a Three-Day-Event and you should find out whether the horse is better suited to a steady trot or prefers a combination of walk and canter. Some horses find it easier to trot the whole way and others finish much fresher by alternating the walk with the canter. The horse breathes in time with the canter pace and therefore the combination of walk and canter should prove to be the better alternative. On the other hand, most horses are capable of trotting at the required speed and it is much easier from the rider's point of view to assess his speed if he is coping with only one pace. You must find out which alternative is the answer for the individual horse.

The jumping practice can be done either at home or away from home. The latter consists of jumping at shows or over someone else's fences or practising over as many types of cross-country obstacles as you can find. In the case of the latter, you should not jump over a full cross-country course but treat each fence as an individual test. The horse is much more likely to learn from his visit if he does it like this and he will pay more attention to what he is doing.

Introduce him to a water splash, as this is a popular fence for course builders and is more than likely to cause the horse trouble if he has never seen one before a competition. Find a stream or a ford with a solid or stony bottom and make the horse walk through it and then up and down in it. Trot into it a few times until the horse is perfectly confident and then erect a very small post and rails in the water. When the horse jumps this fluently, change the position of the fence so that the horse jumps from the bank, over the rail and lands in the water, and then move it again so that he takes off in the water, jumps over the rail and lands on the far bank. Use two fences so that there is one on each bank and then move each fence one stride away from the bank. In this way the horse will be perfectly accustomed to water splash combinations. The main point to remember is that you must never ask the horse to jump into any water where you are not sure that the bottom is perfectly safe and, to make him realise you want him to jump into the water rather than over it, always choose a wide enough stretch which leaves no room for confusion.

Fast work is imperative once the horse has become fairly fit. It clears his wind and prepares him for the effort he will have to make in competition. It is totally unnecessary to work over the distances of the actual event and the graduated gallops as shown on the training chart ensure that he will be fit enough to complete any course without being subjected to great strain. Try to find a straight gallop but, if this is impossible, you must work in the largest field you can find. It is not a good thing for the horse to be galloping on a continual curve. He will change his legs during the fast work and, if he has to turn all the time, this could result in him becoming unbalanced. It is in this sort of circumstance that the horse strikes into himself. It also subjects the horse to too much strain on one side.

Stop work immediately if you see or feel the slightest suspicion of 'a leg'. It will only make matters worse if you think that a few days' slow work will cure the trouble. Take the first signs of heat or swelling as a grave warning and lay the horse off work at once. If you are able to discover the earliest signs of a 'a leg', you may be able to cure it by treating it appropriately and leaving the horse in his box for two or three days. Cut down his food and he will take little harm from the enforced rest. It could mean all the difference between losing your horse for the season with a sprain or a strain and competing with him according to plan.

TRAINING PROGRAMME

Dressage	Road Work plus jumping		
		WEEK ONE: (fill in the dates)	
√	√	Mon.	Dressage: ½ hour; Road Work: ½ hour.
√		Tues.	ditto above
		Wed.	ditto above
		Thurs.	ditto above
		Fri.	ditto above
		Sat.	ditto above

Dressage	Road Work plus jumping		
		WEEK TWO: ( )	
		Sun.	Rest Day.
		Mon.	Dressage: ½ hour; Road Work: ¾ hour.
		Tues.	ditto above
		Wed.	ditto above
		Thurs.	ditto above
		Fri.	ditto above
		Sat.	ditto above

Dressage	Road Work plus jumping		
		WEEK THREE: ( )	
		Sun.	Rest Day.
		Mon.	Dressage: ½ hour; Road Work: ¾ hour.
		Tues.	ditto above
		Wed.	ditto above
		Thurs.	ditto above
		Fri.	ditto above
		Sat.	ditto above

Dressage	Road Work plus jumping		
		WEEK FOUR: ( )	
	√	Sun.	Rest Day.
	√	Mon.	Dressage: ½ hour; Road Work: 1 hour.
	√	Tues.	ditto above
	√	Wed.	ditto above
√	√	Thurs.	ditto above — including jumping practice.
		Fri.	ditto above — 1 hour.
		Sat.	ditto above

Dressage	Road Work plus jumping		
		WEEK FIVE: ( )	
		Sun.	Rest Day.
		Mon.	Dressage: ½ hour; Road Work: 1 hour.
		Tues.	ditto above
		Wed.	ditto above
		Thurs.	ditto above — including jumping practice.
		Fri.	ditto above — 1 hour.
		Sat.	ditto above

Dressage	Road Work plus jumping or gallop.			

WEEK SIX: (   )

Dressage	Road Work plus jumping or gallop.		Day	
			Sun.	Rest Day.
√	√		Mon.	Dressage: $\frac{1}{2}$ hour; Road Work: $1\frac{1}{4}$ hours.
√	√		Tues.	ditto above
√	√		Wed.	ditto above
√	√	√	Thurs.	ditto above — including jumping practice.
			Fri.	ditto above — $1\frac{1}{4}$ hours.
			Sat.	ditto above

WEEK SEVEN: (   )

Dressage	Road Work plus jumping or gallop.		Day	
	√		Sun.	Rest Day.
			Mon.	Dressage: $\frac{1}{2}$ hour; Road Work: $1\frac{1}{4}$ hours.
			Tues.	ditto above
			Wed.	ditto above
√	√	√	Thurs.	ditto above — including jumping practice.
			Fri.	ditto above — $1\frac{1}{4}$ hours.
			Sat.	ditto above

WEEK EIGHT: (   )

Dressage	Road Work plus jumping or gallop.		Day	
			Sun.	Rest Day.
			Mon.	Dressage: $\frac{1}{2}$ hour; Road Work: $1\frac{1}{2}$ hours.
			Tues.	ditto above
			Wed.	ditto above
			Thurs.	ditto above — including jumping practice.
			Fri.	ditto above — $1\frac{1}{2}$ hours.
			Sat.	ditto above

WEEK NINE: (   )

Dressage	Road Work plus jumping or gallop.		Day	
			Sun.	Rest Day.
	√		Mon.	Dressage: $\frac{1}{2}$ hour; Road Work: $1\frac{1}{2}$ hours.
√	√	√	Tues.	ditto above — including gallop: $\frac{3}{4}$ mile at half speed.
			Wed.	ditto above — $1\frac{1}{2}$ hours
			Thurs.	ditto above — including jumping practice.
			Fri.	ditto above — including gallop: $\frac{3}{4}$ mile, half speed.
			Sat.	ditto above — $1\frac{1}{2}$ hours.

WEEK TEN: (   )

Dressage	Road Work plus jumping or gallop.		Day	
			Sun.	Rest Day.
			Mon.	Dressage: $\frac{1}{2}$ hour; Road Work: $1\frac{3}{4}$ hours.
			Tues.	ditto above — including gallop:– (i) $\frac{3}{4}$ mile at half speed. (ii) $\frac{1}{2}$ mile at three-quarter speed.
			Wed.	ditto above — $1\frac{3}{4}$ hours.
			Thurs.	ditto above — including jumping practice.
			Fri.	ditto above — including gallop: $\frac{3}{4}$ mile at three-quarter speed.
			Sat.	ditto above — $1\frac{3}{4}$ hours.

Dressage	Road Work plus jumping or gallop.		

WEEK ELEVEN: (   )

		Day	
		Sun.	Rest Day.
		Mon.	Dressage: $\frac{1}{2}$ hour; Road Work: $1\frac{3}{4}$ hours.
		Tues.	ditto above — including gallop:– (i) $\frac{3}{4}$ mile at half speed. (ii) $\frac{1}{2}$ mile at three-quarter speed.
		Wed.	ditto above — $1\frac{3}{4}$ hours.
		Thurs.	ditto above — including jumping practice
		Fri.	ditto above — including gallop: 1 mile, half speed.
		Sat.	ditto above — $1\frac{3}{4}$ hours.

WEEK TWELVE: (   )

		Day	
		Sun.	Rest Day.
		Mon.	Dressage: $\frac{1}{2}$ hour; Road Work: 2 hours.
		Tues.	ditto above — including gallop, 1 mile at three-quarter speed.
		Wed.	ditto above — 2 hours.
		Thurs.	ditto above — including jumping practice.
		Fri.	Travel to the Event. Dressage and Riding-in.
		Sat.	THE FIRST ONE-DAY-EVENT.

Weeks Thirteen, Fourteen, Fifteen and Sixteen up to a Three-Day-Event continue in the same pattern, but the Road Work remains at two hours' maximum. Following a Three-Day-Event your horse will want a very easy week with only gentle exercise. He will then be ready to return to the training routine for the remainder of the season.

FEED CHART

WEEKS ONE TO FOUR INCLUSIVE: (12 lb. oats equivalent)

7 a.m.
   3 lb. Spillers Racehorse Cubes or horse chow

1 p.m.
   3 lb. Rolled Oats or 3 lb. Spillers Racehorse Cubes or horse chow

6 p.m.
   3 lb. Rolled Oats
   1½ lb. Broad Bran
   1 measure blood tonic
   1 measure cod liver oil
   ½ tablespoon Iodised Salt
   ¾ pint cold water

10 p.m.
   3 lb. Rolled Oats
   1½ lb. Broad Bran
   ½ tablespoon Iodised Salt
   ¾ pint cold water

WEEKS FIVE TO EIGHT INCLUSIVE: (14 lb. oats equivalent)

7 a.m.
   3 lb. Spillers Racehorse Cubes or horse chow

1 p.m.
   3 lb. Rolled Oats or 3 lb. Spillers Racehorse Cubes or horse chow

6 p.m.
   4 lb. Rolled Oats
   1 lb. Broad Bran
   1 measure blood tonic
   1 measure cod liver oil
   ½ tablespoon Iodised Salt
   ¾ pint water

10 p.m.
   4 lb. Rolled Oats
   1 lb. Broad Bran
   ⅓ tablespoon Iodised Salt
   ½ pint water

7 a.m.
   3 lb. Spillers Racehorse Cubes or horse chow

1 p.m.
   3 lb. Rolled Oats or 3 lb. Spillers Racehorse Cubes or horse chow

6 p.m.
   5 lb. Rolled Oats
   $\frac{3}{4}$ lb. Broad Bran
   1 measure blood tonic
   1 measure cod liver oil
   $\frac{1}{2}$ tablespoon Iodised Salt
   $\frac{1}{2}$ pint cold water

10 p.m.
   5 lb. Rolled Oats
   $\frac{3}{4}$ lb. Broad Bran
   $\frac{1}{2}$ tablespoon Iodised Salt
   $\frac{1}{2}$ pint cold water

REST DAYS: (increase hay ration to 10 lb. if below this)

7 a.m.
   2 lb. Rolled Oats
   1 lb. Broad Bran
   $\frac{1}{2}$ tablespoon Iodised Salt
   $\frac{3}{4}$ pint cold water

1 p.m.
   3 lb. Spillers Racehorse Cubes or horse chow

6 p.m.
   4 lb. Rolled Oats
   $1\frac{1}{2}$ lb. Broad Bran
   1 measure blood tonic
   1 measure cod liver oil
   $\frac{1}{2}$ tablespoon Iodised Salt
   $\frac{3}{4}$ pint cold water

CHAPTER EIGHTEEN

Horsemastership. The daily routine. Attention to detail

'Under the eye of the Master, the Horse grows fat.'
(Arabian proverb)

Horsemastership is of vital importance to the well-being of the horse. It is not enough to give him the right amount of work or even to have trained him along the correct lines. He must be studied carefully as an individual both in and out of the stable and all his idiosyncrasies should be noted and analysed. A content horse, in a state of mental and physical well-being, will show this in his general attitude and condition. His eye will be clear and bright, he will be alert and cheerful, his coat will shine from within and he will patently enjoy his work.

The horsemaster's job is to see first that the horse attains this superb state of mental and physical health and then that he maintains it. He must constantly supervise the feeding, grooming and stable management of the horse and know his charge so well that he is immediately aware of the slightest change as soon as it occurs.

As a good horsemaster, you will make sure that the horse is well housed, well fed, well groomed and well looked after in every possible way. You will pay attention to the smallest details and take the extra bit of trouble that makes all the difference. Again and again, circumstances will occur when the horse needs attention at an inconvenient time. It is only too easy to postpone this treatment until it suits you to deal with it, but by then it may be too late. Prevention is far better than cure and this applies to all sorts of situations from the first signs of a horse 'breaking out' after exercise to dealing with the little cut discovered late or a slight swelling which presages leg trouble. So many of the difficulties to which horses are subject can be avoided by prompt action and it should be the maxim of every horsemaster never to put off what he knows should be dealt with at once.

The horse's loose box should be well-aired and large enough for him to lie down in comfort and safety. There should be plenty of clean bedding and his manger and water bucket should be scrubbed out twice a week. See that the horse is properly mucked out each morning before he returns from exercise. He must be encouraged to rest and relax in his stable and if he has a proper bed waiting for him he will soon develop the good habit of lying down in the afternoon after his lunch-time feed. Routine is all-important and once the horse realises the daily pattern he will know that he is left alone for this period of the day and will use it for rest and relaxation.

The day starts with the first feed. Water should be available to the horse at all times except for when he returns from exercise. He must be allowed to cool down thoroughly before he has a proper drink and the most he can have before this is three or four swallows just to moisten his mouth and throat. He should be left alone to eat his first feed and, depending on whether or not you combine the duties of groom and rider, the mucking out takes place either before feeding or when the horse has gone out for his morning exercise. Clean out his feet carefully after breakfast and brush them with hoof oil. 'Quarter' the horse next. This means you give him a cursory grooming just so that he looks clean and tidy to go out. If he wears bandages in the stable, take them off. Do not drop the sheet cotton in the straw where it will pick up bits but smooth it out ready to put back on the horse when he comes back to the stable. Roll up the bandages and leave them with the cotton in a clean place. If the horse wears brushing boots, fasten them on carefully, put on the saddle and bridle and the horse is ready for work.

The tack the horse wears requires constant attention. As soon as he returns to the stable and the tack is taken off, wash the bit so that it will be easy to clean later. Undo the saddle pad from the saddle and place it where the underside will dry properly, and if the horse is wearing brushing boots, put them also out to dry. If the boots are wet and covered with mud, you should let them dry before carefully brushing off the mud. The straps need soaking with saddle soap when you clean the tack. It is advisable to have two sets of boots as sometimes the padding on them takes a long time to dry. It is easier to have the second set to use on alternate days, for the horse is apt to get sore legs if he wears wet boots. They stick to his shins and rub. The tack should be cleaned at the end of every day and repaired at once if the stitching is beginning to work loose. As the horse gets fitter and loses a little weight from his back, the saddle will lie closer to him. Keep a constant check that it does not get too low in front. This can give him a sore back very quickly and even make him go lame. The saddle must remain a perfect fit throughout the training. A standing martingale should never be used, but for jumping and cross-country a running martingale, correctly fitted, can be a useful aid. In principle, the horse should be perfectly obedient at all times and therefore have no need of such artificial aids but there are occasions when he throws his head just at the wrong moment. The running martingale helps to prevent this and whilst it should not be used as a permanent aid, it is there to keep the horse's head down at a crucial moment.

Brushing boots and over-reach boots are a sensible addition to the horse's tack. They protect against all sorts of injuries and should be worn whenever the horse is jumping or on fast work. Some horses are inclined to strike into themselves, particularly on their joints and, if relevant shoeing does not correct this tendency, boots should be worn whenever the horse is out of his stable. Brushing boots must be a good fit or they will cause, rather than prevent, trouble. Each boot must fit snugly well under the horse's knee so that the whole of the cannon bone is supported and protected. Rubber over-reach boots are a must for cross-country work and are to be recommended for show jumping, and the lightweight type will not restrict the horse in any way. Tacking up with boots every day and looking after them properly takes extra time but it is yet another instance of allowing commonsense to take the place of laziness or apathy. It is far better and easier to prevent an injury rather than to cure it.

The horse's pores open while he is out on exercise and he should be strapped as soon as he returns to the stable so that he gains the maximum benefit from this grooming. The first job is to replace the stable bandages if the horse wears them. Most horses are subject to windgalls—especially above the hind joints—when they start serious dressage work and you can prevent these from developing into anything serious by the use of stable bandages. These are not a tight support but are carefully and smoothly applied stockinette bandages over smooth sheet cotton. They cover the legs from knee or hock down to the coronet band. Great care must be taken not to bandage too tightly. The aim is to keep the legs warm and to increase the circulation to the lower limbs and joints. Clean the legs first as soon as you return to the stable, and making sure they are perfectly dry, put on the bandages before you do anything else. It is important not to delay as the legs tend to swell once the horse has been standing for a while. Immediate bandaging will prevent this and keep the legs clean and taut.

Grooming or strapping should be very thorough. After cleaning him first with the dandy brush and then with the body brush and the rubber, the horse's eyes, mouth, sheath and dock should be wiped with a damp cloth and his feet oiled round the wall of the hooves and on the soles. If you make this a daily rule, you are unlikely to miss any foreign matter picked up on exercise, and it can be removed before it has time to affect the horse. The sheath should be cleaned out with warm, soapy water once a week and although the horse may object to this at first he will soon allow you to wash him properly if you are gentle and tactful in your approach.

The muscles on his neck, his shoulders and his quarters can be built up by 'banging'—a form of massage. You use a stable rubber, folded conveniently, and apply it forcefully in a sweeping, glancing movement, along the line of the horse's neck under his mane. The shoulder muscles in question are the bunch of muscles above the horse's forearm, and the quarters are 'banged' on the fleshy part at the top. The sweeping, glancing movement is the key to success. On no account must you 'bang' his rib cage or the area of his loins.

In hot weather and at a certain stage in the training programme the horse will be liable to break out into a sweat after exercise. This may happen as soon as he is back in his box or, if you are unlucky, when he has been in for some time and even after he has been groomed. Never allow him to grow cold and wet with the sweat, for he can easily catch a chill this way. It means more work but you must be prepared to walk him round until he is dry or to towel him until the sweat has gone. Washing down with cold water as soon as the horse returns to the stable is a good preventative. The horse takes no harm as long as the weather is suitable and he is thoroughly dry before he is groomed and put back in his box.

You must make sure he is always rugged up in accordance with the weather. There are days in the winter when the weather suddenly improves and, just like us, the horse may find it too hot under a rug and two blankets. Adapt his clothing to the temperature and do not insist on him wearing too much just on account of the time of year. Conversely, in summer there will be occasions when it turns cold and the horse will benefit from having a rug on him rather than a cotton sheet. You must use your commonsense to deal with the problem.

The feeding time-table should be carefully worked out so that the horse's exercise and grooming can be completed easily before the lunch-time feed. Variety is an important part of feeding and the horse can be given a few chopped carrots or apples on occasions in his feed to stimulate appetite and interest. No hay should be given before the morning work but the horse can have one third of his ration waiting for him when he comes in. The remaining two thirds should be given at tea time when the stables are set fair for the night. After this, he is fed again at ten o'clock, any droppings are picked up and his water bucket checked. The rugs should be straightened before the horse is left.

Use the finest quality oats, bran and hay you can buy and try to keep the horse on the same oats and hay for the whole of the training period. Iodised salt and glucose and mineral licks provide the horse with the opportunity of making whatever he lacks in his diet. His taste will vary according to the state of his constitution and you can either provide several lick holders in his box or change one for another continually. Iodised salt is added to the horse's food, also a blood tonic which contains the extremely valuable vitamin B 12—and daily cod liver oil. All these additives are not only very beneficial but palatable as well. The two feeds of Racehorse Cubes or horse chow, alternating with the bran and oats, help to vary the daily diet and, as such, are very valuable additions. Most horses like boiled feeds, and oats and linseed twice a week with a little barley once a week, gives a real bloom to the coat and keeps condition on the horse. The night before his rest day, he should have a bran mash, and on the actual day he should be given only three instead of four feeds. This gives his stomach a rest on a day when he does not need four feeds. It also helps to keep him on his feed.

There will be times when the horse loses interest in eating altogether and in these cases it does not pay to tempt his appetite with various titbits. It is far better to remove any food that has been left in the manger, scrub it out so that it is perfectly clean, and let the horse miss the next two or three feeds. It will do him no harm and he will be back on his food without any fuss. As a preventative against the horse going off his feed, you should give him a daily dose of a good tonic—your vet can recommend one—which will stimulate his appetite and encourage him to continue to do well. Don't use such a tonic within fourteen days of an event, however, as it contains a substance which would contravene the rules. It is perfectly safe to use up to this time and will be extremely beneficial to the horse. There are also other useful additives your vet may suggest to keep the horse in top condition, with particular usefulness in clearing the wind and serving as a pick-me-up when added to his drinking water the night after an event.

Apart from these general points, you must take particular care of the horse's legs. You must know the potential trouble areas and watch them carefully. All the time you must try to prevent rather than cure. The days of jumping practice or fast work are most likely to affect the legs adversely and you should inspect the horse even more carefully than usual on those evenings. At the slightest sign of swelling or heat, make a thorough examination of the leg or legs concerned. Apply a cooling lotion or a hot poultice of kaolin or Thorpak, according to the nature of the injury, but be sure you have made the right diagnosis of the trouble and are treating the place correctly. If you are in any doubt, call in your veterinary surgeon.

It is a sensible precaution to use a cooling lotion after every gallop. The horse may not actually need it for most of the time but it is a measure well worth adopting for the occasion when it will be of value. Again, it does no harm and will keep the legs in perfect condition.

Horsemastership applies to anything and everything connected with the horse's welfare. If you are really serious in your intention to reach the top in the competitive world, you must take the trouble to become a first class horsemaster. No point is too small to be ignored. Only this constant attitude will produce ultimate and consistent success.

CHAPTER NINETEEN

Preparing for the event. Getting yourself fit. Hints on riding the dressage test. What to take, when to arrive

It is not only the horse who must be fit for the events. You, also, must be equal to the physical strain involved, especially if you have to drive the horsebox and be your own groom. You will not be able to give the horse all the help he needs if you are tired, so you must be fit enough to walk the course twice, inspect and learn the show jumping course and then to work your horse for as long as is necessary the day before the event—all without it being a big effort. Even after you have ridden the horse, he still has to be groomed, his tack cleaned and everything put ready for the morrow's event. You may have to be up early in the morning to groom and plait ready for the dressage test and you should know your times and be thoroughly well-organised in a plan for the whole day. Nothing is more upsetting for the rider on the day of the competition than to discover that a vital piece of equipment has been forgotten or that not enough time has been allowed for the journey or working the horse. You must be in a fit state mentally and physically before you can hope to produce your best form.

As far as personal fitness is concerned, you can prepare yourself for some weeks previous to the event by running or skipping. This applies even more to the person who is able only to ride and who does none of the physical work involved in looking after the horse. The daily riding helps to get you fit but a greater degree of fitness is really necessary to ensure that you are able to give the horse maximum assistance. Running exercise develops your stamina and makes you fit and hard but it requires a great deal of will-power to set off on a daily run in all sorts of weather. It is far easier to skip at home, and ten minutes with the rope each day has exactly the same effect as running and is a much less traumatic experience. Start with only a few minutes skipping and increase the time gradually to the ten minutes' period.

Many people advocate running, not only to get themselves fit initially, but to prepare them for phase C of a Three-Day-Event. They dismount after the steeplechase phase and run alongside their horses for the first few minutes of C. No doubt this is an excellent idea if you are very athletic and can guarantee to dismount and remount without a check and are able to run beside the horse with no consequent lessening of your physical powers. Unless you can manage all this and still remain cool and calm, it is not worthwhile. The horse will recover his breath in the first kilometre if he is allowed to walk on a loose rein with no interference and no shifting of your weight. If he has been well prepared he will be very fit and the difference of weight you achieve by dismounting for a few minutes is not going to be worth the trouble involved. There is also the danger of loosing the horse's rein and the whole exercise is fraught with unwarranted risk.

Although your horse will have learned all the movements demanded in the dressage test, he must be accustomed to working in an actual dressage arena. You must mark out the correct size arena at home and be sure that you know the test perfectly. Take no chances about this as there is nothing worse than suffering a complete loss of memory in the middle of your dressage test. Inevitably, you lose the pattern of the test, the judge has to correct you and advise you of the next movement, and your coolness and concentration are bound to be affected. One mistake leads easily to another and a third mistake means elimination. You must guard against this possibility by learning the test well in advance and riding through it in the arena at home until you know it perfectly. Ride the test either on another horse or on your own competition horse at a walk or a trot so that he has no chance to learn it for himself. Recite the movements and paces to yourself if you are riding the test at one pace. As often as possible, ask a friend to listen to you and to check you with the dressage sheet whenever you have a few moments to spare. You must practise entering the arena from A to C on a mowed or raked strip so that the horse will be accustomed to trotting straight along it and will not shy from a cross at X or a large dot at G.

A sketchy salute at the beginning and end of a test makes a bad impression on the judge. If it is hurried it looks either as if the rider is not confident that his horse will remain in the halt or that he is personally self-conscious about the salute and wants to get it over as quickly as possible. A good first impression goes a long way towards earning good marks so practise your entry and halt and make as much as you can of your salute to the judges. Make sure your back is straight and your head held high as you come in. Establish a square halt, take the reins in your left hand and, if you are a man, take off your hat in a long, sweeping gesture. Replace the hat equally smoothly, take the reins in both hands, make sure the horse is on the bit with combined effect, and move off on a straight line. If you are a woman you have to bow to the judges and, although this does not give you the scope afforded by taking off your hat or giving a smart military salute, it can be made business-like and impressive. Take your reins in your left hand. Take the right arm in a clear and precise movement so that it lies in a straight line parallel with your body. Bow slowly from the hips with your back straight and your head low. Let it be a graceful, un-hurried gesture, then straighten up, bring your right hand back to the reins and prepare to move off from the halt.

The judges are very conscious of the horse's straightness on the long sides of the arena and if you do not watch the quarters care-fully you will lose marks for allowing them to swing even slightly to the inside or to the outside. In the canter transitions you should show a little inside flexion as without this it looks to the judge as if the horse's head is slightly bent to the outside. This applies par-ticularly when you are going away from the judge. Show correct length bend on the circles and in all the corners and turns and ride the test with accuracy and confidence.

Your show jumping preparation has by now been completed by taking part in the available and convenient local show jumper classes and your horse should be capable of negotiating the course at an event with comparative ease. The show jumping phase is not difficult but it is a phase often neglected and valuable marks are thrown away because of inadequate preparation. It is up to you to put in the necessary practice beforehand.

The preparation for the cross-country phase cannot cover all possibilities, but if the horse has been introduced to all the usual fences, and he jumps willingly over ditches and over water, can cope with the different distances in combinations and has seen a water splash, you should have no real problems. The horse will learn more as he competes in the actual events.

Several days before you leave home for an event you should make sure that the horse's shoes are not worn thin and that the thread in the stud holes is unimpaired. Check also that his tack is in good order and that nothing needs to be repaired. You should draw up a list of all the things you will have to take on your journey and check that everything is available. It is not easy to think of what will be wanted at the last minute—this is a sure way of leaving something behind—and it is a good idea to have a permanent list which can be used as a basic guide for each event. In the majority of cases, participation in any event involves a considerable journey and an overnight stay. At the very least you will need fodder for the horse, two haynets, a water bucket and a feed tin. You will

E

want a brush, a fork and a shovel for cleaning out the loosebox and the horsebox, and a muck-sack. Then there is all the horse's tack, his boots, bandages and rugs. He will need to be washed down after the cross-country so you want two more buckets, a sponge, a scraper, some towels and a string vest to go under his rug. The grooming kit, plaiting kit, stud box, hoof oil kit, water carriers and a first aid box are all necessities. Always carry spare bandages, sheet cotton and a variety of cloths and towels, and disinfectant and healing oils to clean out any cuts or wounds plus an Auromycetin spray. It may be that you will need a kaolin poultice, a Thoropak or even a colic drench. Try to think of every eventuality and provide for it. Ask your farrier for a spare set of shoes and keep them permanently in the horsebox. You can lose a shoe at the most awkward times at an event and if you have a spare set with you it may make all the difference to being able to complete the competition.

Check all the things you will have to take for your own personal use. Your dressage and show jumping clothes are the same but you need a sweater for cross-country and a safety helmet. You need a long whip for dressage schooling and another shorter one to use in the show jumping and cross country phases. Check your spurs and take a spare pair of straps in case the other pair are not smart enough to wear for a competition or they get wet the day beforehand and will not brush up into a shine. You must be as clean and tidy as possible and equally as well-turned out as the horse. It takes only a little extra effort and application to appear in a well-brushed coat, clean breeches with a clean white shirt and stock, and shining boots, but it is all very much worth while. A beautifully turned out horse and rider are pleasing to the eye and give the impression that they know their job. Decide to keep up a high standard both for your horse and yourself.

The day before you leave home, see if your horse needs to be trimmed. Remove the whiskers from around his muzzle and his eyes. Trim the hair off his legs and from his withers, and tidy up his ears. Check that his mane and tail are well pulled and clean and that his whole appearance is neat and tidy. If necessary, shampoo his mane and tail with Dermoline. Horse and rider must appear at their very best on the day.

Plan the journey well in advance and decide how long it will take you to travel to the location of the event. Allow plenty of time and arrive either well before the close of declarations or send a letter or telegram to reach the secretary before the specified hour. Generally you should aim to arrive in the early afternoon of the day before the event. This gives you time to declare your horse, walk the courses carefully, work-out and find your allocated stabling well before evening. In this way you will avoid any rush or panic and you will be more able to concentrate fully on the actual competition.

CHAPTER TWENTY

The one-day-event. Walking the course. Preparation
for the competition. Afterwards

In England the order of phases of a One-Day-Event differs from
that of a Three-Day-Event. At most One-Day-Events the cross-
country is the last of the three phases. This is far easier for the
horse and much more convenient for the rider or groom. The horse
will jump in the arena with greater care if he has not already been
over the cross-country course at speed. The show jumping requires
precision and accuracy and perfect bascule, whereas in the cross-
country the horse jumps at speed and therefore does not jump as
cleanly as in the show jumping phase. The sequence with cross-
country as the last phase in a One-Day-Event also helps the rider
or groom. The horse is washed down thoroughly after the cross-
country and it is easier to be able to complete this routine un-
hurriedly, to bandage the horse with a cooling lotion and to make
him comfortable and then to put him away for the day. In the few
instances where the show jumping is the last phase of a One-Day-
Event, it is important to work the horse systematically over the
practice fences before the final phase so that the horse appreciates
that he must jump carefully and cleanly.

Your first move on arriving at the location of the Event is to go
to the secretary's office and confirm that your horse is a runner.
Collect a programme before you start out to walk the cross-
country course. It is only too easy to miss a fence or to take the
wrong part of an alternative if there is more than one class, and you
must check your route carefully as you walk the course. Make sure
you know which coloured markers apply to the obstacles for your
class and concentrate on the individual fences and then the overall
pattern. Take particular notice of the terrain and the approach to
each fence. See if the going varies over the course and remember
where it is good and bad. A small obstacle can present enormous
difficulties if it is cunningly sited and you must assess how each
individual fence should be jumped and at what speed. Generally
speaking, the more straightforward fences may be jumped safely
at an angle if it will save time, but you should not take unnecessary

risks when the acute angle you attempt makes the fence far wider or more difficult than it would otherwise be.

If the horse is running for the first time it is wise to give him every chance of a trouble free début and to take the easiest way round. Depending on his temperament the horse will either take to it quietly and sensibly or he will become highly excited by the proceedings and begin to pull and be difficult to manoeuvre and to place at the fences. In the case of the latter type of horse, his first run over a cross-country course is very important and he will be far more likely to settle sensibly to his new job if you take him slowly and resist the temptation to ride for a place or to demonstrate how fast you can go over the course. You have to realise that there is nothing clever in galloping at full speed round a cross-country course with the horse doing all the work.

Young riders, in particular, seem to think that this is the main objective, and at every event you see horses scrambling over fences when they have been brought into them at a ridiculous speed or an impossible angle. Horse and rider remain upright solely by the grace of God, and a round of this sort—regardless of the fact that it may result in a fast time—is no reason for pride or self-satisfaction. The horse should indeed help himself to a certain extent over the cross-country but the rider is there to give him the best possible chance of success and to complete the course with none of the experiences which may make the horse wary on his next time out. If you continue to ride over the cross-country at a fast gallop without being in complete control, you will inevitably be riding for a fall. One day your luck will change, and the horse will fail to extricate himself from the position in which your bad riding has placed him. At a fast speed and over fixed obstacles your fall will not be pleasant and you will be fortunate to emerge with yourself and your horse unscathed.

Speed is a very important factor but it is something which should develop along with the horse's experience. It must be controlled and you must be able to dictate to the horse exactly how fast or how slowly he jumps a particular part of the course. The horse must learn to listen to you throughout the course and to respond immediately to your demands. If he has been well trained and has complete confidence in you as a rider, his cross-country début will be trouble free. He will know that you ask nothing of which he is incapable.

Do not be upset and think your horse is no good if he stops at an awkward fence on the cross-country. A single refusal, on occasions, when the horse is an utter novice is not a disaster and does not necessarily mean that the horse lacks courage or boldness. Many leading eventers have stopped at a strange fence early in their careers and some of them have even been eliminated. Once again, you have to assess the situation carefully. Has the horse stopped simply because it is the sort of fence he has never seen before or because he met it on entirely the wrong stride? In this case he should jump it the second time. Has he stopped because it is a trappy combination and he does not know how to negotiate it? In this case you have not done enough preparation at home. Or has he stopped out of sheer cussedness and simple non-co-operation when you know he is perfectly capable of jumping the fence? Then he must be taught a lesson. He has to realise he must do exactly as he is told. He must be punished—at the fence, and only at the fence—and with great discrimination. He has to learn that it is far more comfortable to co-operate. This is the lesson he should have learned early in his training.

You must bear in mind all these points when walking the course. Assess the individual fences and decide where the problems lie. Make up your mind how you intend to negotiate each fence and stick to this decision even if you learn that other competitors will jump it in an entirely different way. You know your horse and how he jumps and you should be able to decide on the track best suited to his ability and temperament. Measure the distances carefully in any combination fences and decide the necessary speed of approach to negotiate the obstacle with easy intervening strides. Take especial notice of the composition of fences made up of several elements. In the case of a refusal or a run out you must know whether the fence is marked as two or three separate problems or as several parts of one fence. This will affect how you make a second attempt. A combination fence marked 1A and 1B, or 1A, 1B and 1C is judged as one obstacle and you are allowed only two refusals, runs-out or circles before you are eliminated. If you refuse at any part of the combination you can either attempt to jump from the element where you had a stop or you can retake the whole obstacle 1A and 1B, or 1A, 1B and 1C. Fences marked 1 and 2, or 1, 2 and 3, although sited very close together, are judged separately, and you are allowed two refusals at each obstacle before elimination. You must not retake the first obstacle if you refuse at the second, nor can you re-take any part you have already jumped without incurring elimination.

Make sure you are absolutely clear whether the combination fences are marked as one fence or as separate fences. Although you must never expect nor ride for a refusal, you should know exactly how to complete a combination after a first or even a second disobedience. Look very carefully at the combination and, according to how it is numbered, decide on your walk round the alternative approaches for your second and third attempts. This is very important as it is too easy to ask the horse an impossible question when trying to extricate yourself in the middle of a combination fence.

Whenever the course includes a water splash you must study the approach carefully so that the horse is given every chance of arriving at the fence completely balanced with the water well in sight. Do not be content to judge the depth of the splash by prodding the bottom with a stick. Take the trouble to paddle in it and to make absolutely sure that your chosen line has a sound and level bottom from entry to exit.

After walking the cross-country, inspect the show jumping course and assess this with equal care. Notice whether or not the turns are tight and how best to ride the fences if they are out of line. Pace the distances between combination fences and learn the sequence of the obstacles and their composition so that you can visualise the whole course without looking at it. You must know the cross-country in the same way and be able to ride over each fence in your imagination, knowing how to approach each obstacle and at what speed to negotiate it. You may have to walk the cross-country a second time to make sure of this but it will depend on the time available and how difficult it seems to you. If it worries you a great deal, walk it again. It lessens in size the more you see of it. Beware of the occasions when the course seems too simple. The danger then will be your lack of concentrated effort and the consequent possibility of an unnecessary mistake. The only easy courses are those you have jumped.

The next job is to work your horse. It is best done at the location of the event as it gives the horse an opportunity of seeing the place and he will be less likely to be excited by the strange surroundings the following day. Work him through his dressage routine as near as you can get to the actual arenas. Do nothing to make him think it an exciting place. Your aim is to keep him calm and obedient and totally responsive to your aids. Continue to ride him quietly for an hour or more until he has relaxed and is producing good work.

The starting times for the dressage, show jumping and cross-country may be available by the time the horse is back in the horsebox. If it is too early, you must remember to telephone the secretary at the allotted time that evening. The horse should be settled in his overnight loosebox as soon as possible. Make sure he has plenty of bedding and that there is nothing in the box which could hurt him. He should be well groomed and his stud holes cleaned out and tapped. Plug the holes with oily cotton wool so that the studs will go in easily the next morning. Give the horse his water and a haynet and leave him for half an hour to become used to his surroundings. He can have a small feed as soon as he is settled. If he is a very good doer, he can have his normal tea-time feed.

Meanwhile, the tack has to be cleaned and everything put ready for the competition. If he is to wear bandages instead of brushing boots for the show jumping and cross-country these should be of elastic as they afford good support yet also 'give' on the legs. Cut your sheet cotton ready to go under the elastic bandages and leave them altogether where they will remain perfectly clean. Fill your water carriers so that you are not dependent initially on the supply at the event. You may not have time to go for water the next day and it will conserve that much more of your energy if you have some already in the horsebox. Fill the second haynet. This is for the horse after he has finished the event.

Give him his last feed at ten o'clock and, if you are early in the draw, take away his haynet for the night. Even if you have a late starting time, the horse needs only a little hay. You want his stomach clear of any bulk or he will find it difficult to gallop without stress.

On the morning of the competition, groom the horse, plait his mane neatly and bandage him for the journey. Feed him. Leave the loosebox clean and tidy. Collect your number cloth as soon as you arrive at the location and then get ready for the dressage test. Unplug the stud holes and screw in the studs most suitable for the going. The horse will work in the dressage arena with far more confidence if he is fitted with studs. They give him much more grip on the ground, and he will be able to go deeper into the corners and show more marked changes of pace if he is not afraid of slipping up. Work him through his dressage routine in the same place as the previous day. Remember to take off your tail bandage before you go into the arena and give your horse a final wipe over a few minutes before you are due to start your test.

Go into the dressage ring as the previous competitor is emerging from the arena and trot round the outside of the arena until the judges let you know they are ready for you to start the test. If the judges take a long time between competitors, use this time for a few simple transitions and changes of direction. When the bell rings for you to start your test, make sure your horse is on the bit and responsive to your aids. Make a good approach on a straight line before you enter at A, and smile at the judges as you salute. Try to remain calm and confident throughout the test. There is no need to tense up. You are perfectly prepared and know that you are capable of performing a good test. At the end, having saluted the judges for a second time, leave the arena on a loose rein. Your test is not actually finished until you are out of the arena, so move off from the halt in a straight line and describe a smooth half circle towards the long side. Continue to walk quietly on a loose rein and do not pat your horse or relax your concentration until you emerge at A.

Make much of him and give him some titbit when you dismount, and put him back in the horsebox as soon as he is cool. You can wash out his mouth if he has been very hot but he must have nothing to eat, no hay and no feed. Remove his tack and keep him warm and dry. Make sure you are both ready in plenty of time for the show jumping phase and that you have made the necessary adjustments to the horse's tack. Assume your jumping seat as soon as you mount and the horse will recognise immediately that he has a different job. Find the practice fence in the collecting ring and jump it a few times as an upright and a spread until you are satisfied that he is using himself properly and you have got your eye in for jumping.

The horse must be alert and responsive before he is ready to go into the show jumping ring. He needs a minimum fifteen minutes preparation and probably more than this in his first few events. On the other hand, he will only become bored if you have him out too early. By the time you are due to jump he will have lost interest. Ride the course to the best of your ability and try to follow the exact line you decided upon when you walked the track the previous day. Again, put the horse back in the box as soon as possible and wash out his mouth.

Change into your cross-country sweater and crash helmet and make any additions or alterations necessary to the horse's tack. Leave all the washing down equipment ready for your return. Walk quietly down to the start of the cross-country ten minutes before your time and check that the phase is running to time. If it is, give your horse a short, sharp gallop where you will not interfere with anyone else and then return to the start. This gallop clears the horse's wind and lessens the possibility that he will have to check on the cross-country as he gains his second wind. You are now ready.

The starter will advise you when there are two minutes to go and will then count you down from five seconds. You should be away immediately at a fast canter towards the first fence. Keep calm and ride the horse with determination. Follow the exact track you decided upon and encourage or restrain the horse as and when necessary. Concentrate at every single fence and do not relax until you have passed through the finishing flags. Remember to weigh-in if you have to carry 165 lb. (75 kg.).

The horse will enjoy himself thoroughly if he completes the course without any trouble. Make much of him in this case and continue to bear in mind, despite your elation or your disappointment if he has done badly, that his welfare is your first consideration. Before anything else, you must see that he is made comfortable and you should return straight away to the horsebox. Take off his tack and bandages and wash him down carefully. Look for any little cuts and attend to them. Walk him dry, put on his cotton and bandages with a cooling lotion, his rug with a string vest under it and take out his studs. Load him into the horsebox as soon as you can. His first drink should contain a double handful of glucose powder. This will restore lost energy and keep him contented. He can have his haynet now, and, throughout this entire routine, you should try to convey your pleasure to the horse if he has been a good boy. He will appreciate this and retain his enjoyment of the day's proceedings in retrospect. The sooner he returns home, the more contented he will be. The horse's good efforts must be rewarded and if he is left in the horsebox for an hour or so after he has finished the event with nothing to keep him happy, his enthusiasm will wane. The horse's welfare is your main consideration and you must sacrifice everything else to this aim.

Organise that there is a boiled feed waiting for him on your return home—especially if this is something he really likes. Check him over once more and then leave him in peace for the night. The next day he should be walked out quietly to get rid of any resulting stiffness, and on the following day he can resume his training routine but on a restricted scale. The third day he should be back in full training.

CHAPTER TWENTY-ONE

The three-day-event. When to arrive. The dressage day.
The speed and endurance day. The show jumping day

The final preparation for a Three-Day-Event is the continuation of the routine contained in the twelfth week of the training pro-gramme. The horse needs a further four weeks work after his initial twelve weeks if he is to be fit enough to make a winning effort. He must be at peak fitness for a Three-Day-Event and will have reached this condition only if he has completed the programme without missing more than the odd day's work. In this case, you can be confident of his physical state. He will also be in the correct mental state as long as you have subjected him to no unpleasant experiences during his preparation and that he retains his confi-dence in you both in and out of the stable.

The Three-Day-Event generally takes place from a Friday to a Sunday and a large entry means that some competitors will be required to do their dressage on the Thursday. You will be advised in advance if you are among this minority. The horse should be well settled in before the start of the Event and it is wise to arrive on the Wednesday at the very latest and, preferably, on the Tuesday afternoon. This allows you to work the horse at home in the morning and to give him his last full gallop. You arrive well before the start of the event so that your horse has plenty of time to settle quietly into his new surroundings before the atmosphere becomes electric in anticipation of the competition. If you have been groom and rider up to this point you must arrange to have someone else to look after the horse for the event. It is impossible to combine the duties during a Three-Day-Event, and a would-be-eventer gains valuable experience by acting as groom in these circumstances.

Make sure your horse's shoes are in good order before you leave home and that the spare set is in the horsebox. Check your list carefully so that nothing is left at home. The horse must have his normal exercise on the day or days preceding the event. Make him realise that he is following his ordinary routine and he will be far more likely to settle and to eat up. Try to do nothing to excite or upset him in any way.

There is a conducted tour of the Speed and Endurance course and preceding this all competitors are briefed on specific points relating to the cross-country fences and on general procedure during the event. On no account must you miss this briefing. You will be given a programme and a map of the Speed and Endurance course and then the competitors motor round Phases A and C and walk the steeplechase course. Take particular notice of the compulsory turning flags, or checkpoints, on the Roads and Tracks and mark off the position of the kilometre signs and their total on your map. Study the map carefully to see if there is any possibility of taking a short cut. If you think you can see a shorter way than the route shown you will reconnoitre this when you make a second inspection of the course alone. Assess the steeplechase course carefully. It usually consists of five fences on a circular loop and each fence is jumped twice. You must work out the exact half way point so that you are able to check your speed during the actual competition. By this time you will know the approximate distance your horse covers before he takes his second wind. Remember to bear in mind that he will lose speed fractionally for these few strides.

Walk the cross-country phase simply to gain an overall impression of the composition of the course. It is better to delay a really thorough assessment of each fence and the decision of how to negotiate them until you can give the course your undivided attention. It is not easy to do this if you are accompanied by other competitors. In addition, your horse may need more exercise if he is to do his dressage test the next day and he must finish this and then be groomed and produced in good order for the veterinary inspection in the late afternoon. This inspection is merely a formality unless your horse is patently lame or a little 'footy'. The panel will spin a lame horse but may allow a footy one to complete the dressage phase and will then inspect him again before the Speed and Endurance test. The risks of a Three-Day-Event are great enough on a sound horse and it is extremely foolhardy to invite trouble by starting on an animal whose soundness is suspect. The disappointment is great but it is far better to withdraw under the circumstances and to save the horse for another time.

After the veterinary examination, make sure the stud holes are cleaned out and plugged with new pieces of oily cotton wool and that your groom knows exactly what time you want the horse next day.

DRESSAGE DAY

You know from experience how much work the horse needs before his test so have him out in just enough time to make sure he will be absolutely ready to do a good test. As always, work him through his usual routine, and then wipe him over with a rubber before you go into the arena. Keep cool and calm and try to convey to the horse your sense of confidence.

After the test the horse should have a sharp gallop to clear his wind properly in readiness for the Speed and Endurance test. Put on his boots or bandages and gallop at three-quarter speed over a half mile stretch. Choose a place well away from the dressage area where you will not interfere with competitors still preparing for their tests.

You have the rest of the day to walk the cross-country course again and to see if there is any possibility of a short cut on the Roads and Tracks. Be extremely careful that your route misses none of the checkpoints. This time you walk the cross-country slowly and with great concentration. Your first view of it on the official walk round has already given you a rough idea of the problems involved and you know the general direction of the course and the approach to each fence. Measure the distances between the combinations and decide which line in the alternative fences is best suited to your horse.

If there is a water splash, walk around in it so that you know that your chosen route has a sound bottom and that there are no holes into which the horse might stumble. Take note of the depth of the water and remember that the deeper it is the worse the drag. At a canter a horse cannot free his front legs quickly enough from a depth of more than two feet (61 cm.) and you should approach any water splash at a trot or at a very restricted, controlled and bouncy canter. You should trot through the actual splash and keep the horse together with strong rein contact and driving leg aids. Realise that the horse may be tired towards the end of the course and that you should not then ask him for a greater effort than is ·necessary. If an alternative fence calls for really long intervening strides and a big jump out, or a more careful approach with an extra stride in the middle, you should decide on the latter. In the actual competition, when you find that your horse is far more full of running than you had anticipated, you can ask him for the bigger effort. You must be able to assess the changing capabilities of the horse as you ride round the course and know which alternative is best for him in the circumstances.

Your groom must be well briefed as to her duties on Speed and Endurance day. Make sure she knows where is the start of A and the location of the 'box' or 'pocket'. The 'pocket' marks the finish of C and the start of D and it is here that you take the compulsory halt of ten minutes and are inspected by a committee of one veterinary surgeon and two officials. All the washing down equipment and spare tack is taken to the 'pocket' before the start of the Speed and Endurance phase. Your groom leads the horse to the start of A and then goes to the 'pocket' to await your return off Phase C.

The next task is to work out your times for the Roads and Tracks and the Steeplechase phase and to decide on how long you need in the pocket to prepare for Phase D, the cross-country. You will have the Compulsory Halt time of ten minutes but it is advisable to finish phase C in two minutes less than the optimum time. The optimum times for the Roads and Tracks, the Steeplechase phase and the cross-country are set out in the programme and you will be given a typed sheet showing the competitors' times for all four phases. The optimum times for the Steeplechase and cross-country phases mean no penalty points and to achieve this you have to cover the distances at 26 m.p.h. (690 metres a minute) and 21½ m.p.h. (570 metres a minute) respectively. Your speed on the Roads and Tracks is influenced by the time you decide to deduct from the stated Optimum Time. You cut down this time in order to give the horse a breather before the Steeplechase or to increase the ten minute Compulsory Halt time in the pocket before the cross-country.

Assume the summary of the Speed and Endurance phases is as set out on the sample table below:

SUMMARY OF PHASES										
Phase	Nature	Distance			Speed		Optimum Time		Time Limit	
		Mls.	Yds.	Metres	Yds. per min.	Ms. per min.	min.	sec.	min.	sec.
A	Roads & Tracks	3	484	5280	262	240	22		26	24
B	Steeplechase	2	416	3600	755	690	5	13	12	
C	Roads & Tracks	5	632	8640	262	240	36		43	12
	Vet. Inspection	–	–	–	–	–	10		–	–
D	Cross-country	4	570	6982	624	570	12	15	31	

If the Optimum Time for A, the Roads and Tracks, is twenty-two minutes and the distance to be covered is 5280 metres, you should base your calculations on there being five kilometre marker posts between the start and finish of the phase. You should aim to have four minutes in hand as you finish A so that you have time to check your horse's girth and to make any necessary adjustments to the tack. You will also see the previous competitor completing the course and get an idea of how it is riding. Your groom will not have time to meet you at the end of Phase A, but it is a good idea to arrange for someone else to be there to assist you. The actual distance to be covered on A is more than five kilometres, and if you want to finish in eighteen minutes instead of twenty-two minutes, you should allow three and a quarter minutes for each kilometre. Base all your calculations on a starting time of twelve o'clock. This simplifies what will inevitably be a very complicated time schedule and has the added advantage that any change to your starting time, because of a delay or hold up on the course, has no effect on the time schedule you have worked out for yourself. You merely put back your watch the equivalent number of minutes to the duration of the delay when you check your watch with the starter prior to setting out on A. Phase A is set out to show the exact time you pass each kilometre post and pass through the finish to await being set off on Phase B. The Optimum Time for the Steeplechase phase—no penalty points—is 5 mins 13 secs and you should determine to complete the first circuit in 2 mins 30 secs. Without realising it, you will gallop more slowly the second time round and you need the extra thirteen seconds in hand to avoid penalty points.

The Optimum Time for Phase C commences as soon as you finish the Steeplechase, Phase B, and on C there are eight kilometre markers over a distance of 8640 metres. Make your calculations as if there were 9000 metres or nine kilometres markers, the ninth being the finish of C. The Optimum Time is thirty-six minutes so if you want to save two minutes on the phase you have to complete C in thirty-four minutes. After the Steeplechase the horse will be very much out of breath and he must be walked on a loose rein until he has recovered and is ready to trot and canter on round the phase. You must allow twice as much time for the first kilometre as for any of the others to provide for this recovery. Accordingly, work out the schedule for C as if there were ten sections. The thirty-four minutes are divided by ten and each section is allowed 3 mins 24 secs. Therefore, you can allow yourself 6 mins 48 secs on the first kilometre and then pick up the faster speed, or you can disregard the first kilometre post and allow 10 mins 12 secs for the first two kilometres. By this time your horse should be completely recovered and ready to take up the steady trot pace with an occasional canter or the alternate walk and canter progression.

Your timetable is now complete except for marking the starting time for the Cross-Country phase. This will be twelve minutes after you finish Phase C. You have saved two minutes on C which are added to the ten minutes compulsory halt. Make out two copies of the time schedule on postcards ready to be strapped on your arms before the Speed and Endurance test. Write down the actual starting time for Phase A, the time you intend to finish C and how long you have in the pocket for the business of washing down, and give this to your groom.

TIME SCHEDULE FOR THE SPEED AND ENDURANCE TEST

Start A	12.00	⎫
1 km.	12.03.25 secs.	
2 km.	12.06.30	
3 km.	12.09.45	22 minutes.
4 km.	12.13.00	$3\frac{1}{4}$ mins each kilometre.
5 km.	12.16.15	
Finish A	12.18.00	⎭

In Hand	4.00	

Start B	12.22.00	⎫
$\frac{1}{2}$ way	12.24.30	No Penalties: 5 Mins 13 secs
Finish B	12.27.13	⎭

Start C	12.27.13	⎫
1 km.	12.34.01	
2 km.	12.37.25	
3 km.	12.40.49	
4 km.	12.44.13	
5 km.	12.47.37	34 minutes.
6 km.	12.51.01	
7 km.	12.54.25	
8 km.	12.57.49	
Finish C	13.01.13	⎭

Compulsory Halt	10.00	
In Hand	2.00	
Start D	13.13.13	

Make sure the horse is comfortable, that all the bandages and boots are ready, and that the tack is cleaned. Tell your groom to remove the small haynet at ten o'clock that evening.

The author. Countdown to the start of the Speed and Endurance Phase. Note the two watches on the left wrist to act as a double check for the two phases of Roads and Tracks. On the right wrist, the stop watch set to time the Steeplechase Phase. Also the two copies of the Time Schedule, each copy strapped to a forearm, and the safety pins to prevent the number cloth straps from slipping down over the arms.

Speed and Endurance Day

The first thing to ascertain is whether or not there has been any change in the going since you walked the course. If there has, you should walk parts of it again or, at least, look at the more difficult fences where a deterioration in the going will further complicate the problems. Remember that the going affects the way in which the horse tackles the obstacles and make any new decisions for negotiating them according to the changed conditions. Take the trouble to find out everything possible as to how the early horses on the course are coping with difficult conditions and how it is jumping, but remain calm and resolute and do not be deterred from your own riding plan. Take your saddle and weigh out on the scales in the starter's tent. Tape your time schedules on to your forearms where they can be read easily as you go along. Strap on your watch, preferably one with a large, clear face and a minute hand, and also a military type wrist-stop-watch for use on the Steeplechase phase. It is advisable to carry a third watch as a check and a further precaution.

Make sure all the equipment goes to the pocket. You will need three buckets, two sponges, glucose powder, several towels, four stable rubbers folded crosswise, a string vest and rug, the spare set of shoes, spare girths, a whip, leathers and reins, and a set of boots and bandages. Also a spray for cuts. Apart from the horse's equipment, you will want a thirst quenching drink, an extra pair of gloves, a towel and a coat. All these things must go to the pocket and be placed in an agreed position well before you are due to start.

Make one plait of the horse's mane just behind his ears and tie the bridle on to this. In the case of a fall it lessens the possibility of losing the bridle when it is fixed in this way. Check that the tack is fitted correctly and ask the groom to lead him quietly to the start with a rug on so that the horse is there ten minutes before your time. Ask the starter for a time check and set your watches back from twelve o'clock the same number of minutes that are to elapse before your actual starting time. You are now ready for the Speed and Endurance Test.

There is no need to wake up your horse before the start of Phase A. There will be plenty of time for him to liven up on the Roads and Tracks. Mount him just a few minutes before you are due to start and set off quietly at a trot when the starter lowers his flag. Check your watch every time you pass a kilometre post to see that it coincides with your time schedule and adjust your speed until you find the necessary pace.

At the start of the Steeplechase phase, get ready to press the button on your stopwatch. You must be able to see clearly when the 2 mins 30 secs, which have been allowed for reaching the half way marker, have elapsed. Ride at a strong gallop all round the first circuit, driving well into each fence and asking the horse to stand off and jump out of his stride. The half way marker is generally on the flat and you have plenty of time to start to look at your watch as you approach the spot. If you are under the time and are therefore galloping at too fast a speed, take care not to slow down too much on the second circuit and ultimately finish with penalty points. Remember that your speed will not be as great as you think it is the second time round, and make the necessary allowance for this.

If you are over the time and realise that you could easily have gone faster on the first circuit, increase your speed and try to improve your time on the second loop. Do not push the horse if you feel he is already going as fast as he can. The speed for no time penalties is a fast one over the distance and not all horses are capable of achieving this when going well within themselves and consequently of still having the energy and stamina to complete the rest of the course without stress.

Allow the horse to stop galloping in his own time as you finish Phase B, and try to remember to press the stopwatch as you pass through the finish of the Steeplechase phase. It does not help if you pull at the horse to make him stop. Let him settle gradually to a walk and then sit still and allow him to continue on a loose rein. Once again, check your watch against the kilometre posts and your time schedule. It will seem an age before the horse recovers his breath but stay calm and be patient. He will have recovered by the time you pass the second kilometre post. As you approach the finish of C, allow the inspection committee to see your horse trotting towards them clearly. In all probability they will trouble you no further in the pocket if you give them this chance of seeing that the horse is sound.

Passing through the finish of C, dismount immediately, and start on the routine of preparing the horse for the cross-country. Face the horse into the wind, take the reins over his head, loosen the girths and cover the saddle with a towel. Tie a stable rubber just below the knee of each leg to prevent the bandages being soaked. Sponge him down thoroughly, scrape off the excess water and wipe him with another rubber. Take off the rubbers from each leg. Wipe his face, and wash out his mouth with a clean sponge and a glucose mixture. Remove the towel from the saddle and throw over a string vest. Check the bandages and studs and deal with any cuts. Tighten the girths, put the reins back over his head and he is ready for the cross-country. If you have time to spare, let the horse walk gently up and down in the pocket. You can remove the two extra watches and your time schedules, but keep on the stopwatch in case you are halted on the course. This can be a useful way of confirming the length of time you are held up.

Set off on the cross-country course full of determination and help the horse as much as you can. Stick to your riding plan and approach every fence so that your horse has every chance of jumping it safely. Use your head the whole way round the course. Do not relax for an instant and do not panic if you have a refusal or a fall. Assess the situation and get out of it the best possible way. Take no unnecessary risks, but if your horse is jumping easily and everything feels perfect, press on at a relentless, steady pace. It is infuriating to finish a course with no jumping penalties and know that you have plenty in hand. You have to find the correct balance between going too fast early in the course and having no energy left, and going too steadily throughout and finishing with too much in hand. This is a matter of experience.

As soon as you have finished D, take the horse back to the stables. Wash him down thoroughly and inspect him very carefully for cuts and bruises. You will remember whether or not he hit any fences hard and where the damage is likely to be. Make sure you investigate every possible site of injury and deal with anything you find. Apply a cooling lotion to the horse's legs, give him a glucose drink as soon as he is completely dry and cool and leave him to rest for an hour. Feed him and then take him outside to see that he is still sound. If he shows any signs of lameness and you cannot detect the reason for it, call in the veterinary surgeon. It is his job to help all competitors to produce their horses fit enough to pass the veterinary inspection at ten o'clock the next morning. Return him to his box immediately if he is sound and take a further look at him last thing at night. You may have to work throughout the night to ensure that he is sound enough to pass the inspection panel but if you are lucky your horse will be merely stiff and he will require nothing more than half an hour's led walk before the start of the inspection.

Show Jumping Day
The first objective is to get the horse past the veterinary examination panel. They will spin only the horses that are badly lame and who are patently incapable of jumping. They will pass those one would not normally consider sound but who will obviously not suffer from jumping a small course in the arena. Walk your horse quietly for half an hour before the inspection and make sure

you run him up in front of the panel on a tight rein. The horse can be plaited and tidied up ready for the parade of competitors as soon as he has been passed by the panel, and while this is being done you can inspect the show jumping course and learn it perfectly. Once again, assess its problems carefully and remember that your horse must be a little tired and will not be capable of showing all his usual fluency and athletic ability.

Have the horse led up to the arena ten minutes before the parade and walk him round with the rest of the competitors remaining in the competition. For the weigh-out (required in the United States) you should make sure you are carrying the correct weight of 165 lb. (75 kg.). You must weigh in as soon as you have completed your round in the show jumping arena. After the parade, prepare your horse for the third phase. Throughout the Speed and Endurance Test he was encouraged to stand off the forty-odd fences and negotiate them at speed. Now he must learn to change his approach altogether and to jump the fences in the arena cleanly and with a perfect bascule. He must adjust his jumping to the precision and accuracy required for a clear round.

Use the practice fence to achieve this and allow the horse to jump once or twice as an upright post and rails to make sure that he has lost the stiffness and is responsive to your aids. Then take away the second rail and leave the fence as a single pole with no take off guide. He will probably hit the rail and this should encourage him to try harder next time. Reward him if he makes a better effort at his second attempt and jumps the rail precisely and cleanly. Erect a spread fence and repeat the exercise. The object is to explain to the horse that he is required to make an extra effort. He must jump well over the top of each obstacle instead of jumping with a flatter back as in the steeplechase and cross-country phases.

As your turn approaches, keep the horse alert and his outline short. His hind legs must be well underneath him and he should be perfectly responsive to your aids. Go into the arena and make your salute to the royal box or to the judges. Wait for the signal and then start your round. Follow the usual pattern of keeping to the exact track you decided upon in your inspection of the course and remember that in a Three-Day-Event the course is always twisty and fairly long. You cannot afford to swing out on the corners and turns and you must keep up a steady pace. Ride with quiet determination and a cool head and use all your ability and talent to help the horse. The starting order for the jumping is generally in reverse order of the placings, so that the horse at the bottom of the list is first into the arena and the leading combination jumps last. You will know your final placing almost as soon as you have jumped and the prizes are presented immediately after the leading horse has completed his round.

All that remains is to return the horse to the stables and either to prepare him for the journey home or to unplait him and settle him for a well-earned rest. In both cases he should have a cooling lotion put back on his legs and he should be made comfortable. He will need an easy week at home after the event and should have only walking exercise or given half an hour's grazing every day during this time. Remember to adjust his food accordingly. The following week, if the season continues, he can return once more to the training programme. If the Three-Day-Event is the close of the season, he is roughed off gradually and goes out into the field as soon as the weather permits.

The training season is over.

The author with 'Fair and Square'. Halt. Salute!

'Never thank yourself.
Always thank the horses
For the happiness and the joy
We experience through them.'
              Hans H. E. Iscabart

GLOSSARY OF TERMS

How to make use of the Glossary: having read the item, look up the corresponding entry in the index and then turn to the explanation in the text.

Above the bit—a resistance or evasion as the horse raises his head to escape the action of the bit.

Aids—your means of communication with the horse by the use of hands, legs and the influence of the body. At all times the aids should be clear and consistent. Artificial aids are the voice, the whip and the spur.

Banging—a form of massage. Of immense value in developing the muscles on the neck, the shoulders and the quarters.

Bascule—the perfect arc described by the horse over a fence, using head and neck freely and rounding his back to follow the line of the half circle from take off to landing.

Behind the bit—an evasion when the horse refuses to go up to his bridle and take hold of the bit.

Bloquer—an extremely effective and strong aid to make a transition down from a fast pace to walk or halt.

'Blowing up'—a horse 'blows up' when he is highly excited or in a state of nervous tension. He loses all his calmness and it is impossible for the rider to make him produce any good work.

Bridle lameness—an irregular pace arising not from an unsoundness but from the horse resisting the rider in some way. It can develop if the rider does not remember to change the sitting diagonal regularly at the trot or if he sits unevenly on the horse and applies the legs with unequal pressure.

Cadence—rhythm intensified to absolute perfection.

Carrying capacity of the hocks—The third stage of training. The centre of gravity has moved well back and the quarters are lower than the forehand. The hind leg is engaged well under the horse and he carries his full weight on his hocks.

Combined effect—the simultaneous application of hand and leg aids to achieve direct flexion. The hands are raised, fingers vibrating to soften the horse's mouth, to encourage the horse to relax his jaw and lower his head, and the legs are applied on the girth on the sensory nerves. It is the aid to bring the horse on the bit.

Developing the propelling power of the hocks—The first stage of training. The long and low position, when the horse's head and neck are low and stretched and the centre of gravity is over the forehand. The horse learns to use his hocks and to push freely forwards from behind.

Feeling—a God-given gift to a few who are thereby able instinctively to deal with any of the problems which inevitably arise when training a horse. It can be attained to a certain degree after the establishing of the correct seat.

Four track work—see leg yielding and riding in position.

Half halt—a momentary closing of the hands and legs. Used as a warning to the horse that he will be asked for a transition or change of direction etc. Also has the advantage of temporarily moving the centre of gravity back and therefore encourages 'self-carriage'.

Horsemastership—the art of caring for the horse mentally and physically both in and out of the stable.

Leg yielding—an exercise designed to teach the rider to 'feel' the horse and to show him how to influence the positioning of the horse's head and neck and body.

Length bend—the continual curve throughout the horse's body from nose to tail. Length bend is shown on a circle, a turn or in a corner.

On the bit—the horse is on the bit when he accepts his bit happily and goes freely forward with steady headcarriage.

Renvers or 'Tail to the Wall'—a gymnastic exercise to improve the horse's length bend and suppleness. It confirms his correct bend and improves the rider's ability to position the horse.

Rhythm—the marked regular beat of the movement.

Riding in position—an exercise designed to teach the rider to 'feel' the horse and to show him how to influence the positioning of the horse's head and neck in relation to his body.

Self-carriage—the second stage of training. The horse's hind legs are well under him and his forehand is light and free.

Shoulder-in—a suppling exercise to encourage the horse to activate the inside hind leg and to bring it well under his body. It increases the flexion of the hock.

Simple change of leg—the transition from the canter with one leg leading to the canter with the other leg leading but with two or three intervening walk strides. There must be no trot strides in the transition down to walk or up to canter.

Sitting diagonal—at the rising trot the rider sits as one pair of diagonals meets the ground. The rider should always sit as the inside hind leg meets the ground, called the inside diagonal. This means that on the left rein, the rider sits as the near hind and off fore meet the ground. On the right rein the inside diagonal is off hind and near fore.

Three track work—see shoulder-in.

Travers or 'Head to the Wall'—a gymnastic exercise to improve the horse's length bend and suppleness. It confirms his correct bend in the corners and turns.

Two track work—see Travers and Renvers and half pass.

Überstreichen—the surrender of the hand to demonstrate that the horse remains in self carriage.

Vibrations—a vibratory movement of the fingers alone in a steady hand used to soften the horse's mouth. It is particularly useful in transitions and whenever the horse threatens to resist or evade with his head and neck.

Index